An Island I Don't Want to Be On
Surviving the Riptide of Bipolar Disorder

by W. Hector Rivera

Cover and interior design by Vinnie Corbo
Author photo by Pablo Rivera

Published by Volossal Publishing
www.volossal.com

Copyright © 2024
ISBN 978-1-963359-17-6

This book may not be reproduced or resold in whole or in part through print, electronic or any other medium. All rights reserved.

Publisher's Note

The contents of this book are W. Hector Rivera's personal memoirs of how he experienced and interpreted the events detailed in this book. They are in no way meant to be a historical accounting. The thoughts, opinions and recollections in no way reflect the opinions of the publisher or the characters in the story. This book is intended for entertainment purposes and to educate the public about bipolar disorder and how to live with it.

To my wife, the greatest miracle of my life,
and without miracles, what is left?

And to my daughter;
for teaching me the value of a free spirit.

CHAPTER ONE

As the light turned green and the ambulance pulled forward, from its small window I watched the woman who looked like my wife disappear as we left the front of my house, and thought about wanting a miracle. But I knew that a miracle wasn't coming to me in this ambulance anytime soon.

When we arrived at the facility – and honestly, I don't remember the street – I noticed the big white numbers that read 765. I also noticed the view. From the street, in the background you can see the downtown Los Angeles skyline. It reminded me of the view from Dodger Stadium parking lot, but not as elevated. When my gurney was rolled up to the gate, we had to be buzzed in. It reminded me of the buzz of a prison door when either they let you in to see visitors or released someone who had done their time.

It also reminded me about the summer of my eighth grade year when I decided to spend it with Cookie. August hit, and she ended up getting arrested for drug possession. The fucked up thing about it was that though she was dealing drugs in the apartment, the dope belonged to a teenage runaway named Maria. She brought some coke home and left it on the dresser. I figured that the cops had been trying to bust Cookie all summer for selling heroin, and they couldn't bust her for distribution so they decided to get her on the lesser charge, and what made matters worse, she had outstanding warrants and they took her away immediately. She served three weeks. We went to pick her up at Sybil Brand dentention center, which was near downtown L.A. as well. The front of the prison had a turnabout. From a distance, it did not look like a prison but more like an elementary or middle school, but then you see the huge gates with barbed wire on the top. The building had green poles holding it up. When my Aunt Doris and I pulled up, Cookie walked up to the front gate. My Aunt Doris got out of the car and went to meet her. Once we were at the gate, the gate buzzed, and Cookie was released. That buzzing took me right back to that summer, and I remember how shitty that summer was once that buzzed happened, and I had that same feeling, but it seemed like it was on another level because I was the one going in instead of Cookie.

I waited in the hallway for a while, so keeping track of time was difficult. I don't recall how long I waited but then a young guy, a Registered Nurse, wrote down my information. He took my personal items and put them in a manila envelope. I saw my daughter's volleyball picture fall out of my wallet, and I asked if I could keep it with me. He said, "Yes," but I could not keep my necklace; "for safety reasons," he said. He continued with his paperwork and was a very nice guy, but I couldn't remember anything he was asking me except if I wanted to hurt myself or others. When we were done I looked at him and asked him, "Am I going insane?" He told me in a reassuring way, no, that I was just going through a "very difficult moment."

After I was given a tour, I was given my cholesterol medication and some other medication of which I was unaware. I paced back and forth from my doorway to the small cafeteria that was used as a makeshift art room. I kept doing this, marking off the time on the clock. I really thought I was going to pull my insane-ness out of my system and they were going to let me out of the facility. I got agitated and told the nurse if I did twenty more runs that I would be ready to go home.

He nodded and said, "We'll see," with a serious look on his face.

He then came back and told me that I should go to my room and rest. I refused. I kept pacing so I could keep my routine of walking from my room to the cafeteria. But every time I took a step, a staff member would take one step forward toward me. I paced about ten feet and there was a staff member at each doorway all the way down the hallway. I was too exhausted physically to attempt to push through the staff members, but for a moment I thought about it. At that point, I just got in bed and was surprised how fast I fell asleep. But before I fell asleep, I had a single moment of clarity where I formulated a lucid thought in a form of a question: "How the fuck did I end up here?"

CHAPTER TWO

The phone on my alarm went off. I pressed the snooze button. I knew I had a ten minute buffer. But I once heard a former elite Navy Seal say that one of the worst things you can do is press the snooze button. He said that the snooze button was a dream killer. Ten minutes later, the phone went off again and I muttered, "Fuck!" under my breath. As soon I muttered that, my dog, who was sleeping at the foot of our bed, perked her ears and looked at me like I committed a big time sin. I leaned over and rubbed her ears and apologized.

I looked over at my wife and she was sleeping peacefully. She always did. I'm the one that always struggled with sleep. I wished I could sleep like she looked at this moment. I knew she had about thirty minutes before she needed to get up, so I tried to get out of bed quietly without waking up. It's funny how you try to be careful about something but you make things worse. As I was trying to get carefully out of bed, I bumped my knee into my night stand.

"Shit," I said, grabbing my knee while still trying to be quiet.
"Good morning," said my wife.
"Damn, I'm sorry."
"It's okay, I needed to get up anyway," she said.
"But I know you don't get up for another thirty."
"It's okay, I'll help you get Mar up."
"Good luck with that," I said.

In the past, in wasn't very difficult to get our daughter up in the morning, but *now* we are talking about high school. Getting her up could be monumental. Honestly, I could use the break from having to get her up. So I went to the bathroom to get ready.

I did the usual things; brushed my teeth, flossed, mouthwash, put deodorant on, put product in my hair. That was my mistake. I paid too close attention to putting on the product. I saw my widow's peak. I then noticed some of the gray. But the gray did not bother me as much as the widow's peak. 'Should I just go bald, or maybe grow it out longer and figure out a hairstyle?' I wasn't sure.

I then looked at my gut. I turned to the side. 'What happened to me?' I liked the shape of my shoulders and my arms and my chest. 'If only I can cut the portion from below my chest to my thighs I would be happy.' I know that's a vain thought when there are bigger fish to fry in life, but that's how I felt.

I got over the pipe dream of thinking I can turn back the clock to what I looked like ten or twenty years ago and then continued with my morning routine and I shaved my face. I cleaned myself up and headed back to the bedroom to put on my clothes. I saw my lazy ass dog still lying in bed. I called the dog lazy because I was jealous. I wish I could lie in that bed for most of the day but like a buddy of mine said, "It's back to the salt mines." I wanted to make the bed while my wife was waking up our daughter, but I didn't have the heart to kick my dog off at that point, so I put on my clothes without incident.

I walked toward the kitchen but just before I walked past the hallway into the kitchen I saw the wall of our daughter's school pictures from preschool to high school. I always noticed the pictures but I seem to pause a little longer because she is in high school now, and I know that she'll be off to college in a couple of years and got nostalgic. I looked at all the photos. The wall was my wife's idea. She said her parents did the same thing with her and her brother's yearly school photos. Her and her brother nicknamed it the Wall of Shame. But they got a kick out of it as they both got older and she told me that is what she wanted to do once we had our own children. I looked over the photos a little bit longer. My wife entered the hallway.

"What are you doing?"

"Reminiscing, I guess."

"They're cute," she said.

"Yeah," I said. "Which one do you like?"

"The one where she had braces."

"I like the preschool one. Her little smile and her little black

T-shirt. I'm not saying she's not a happy kid but she is really happy in that photo. Like she knows she's loved. I wish that I could have known what that was like when I was her age."

"I know," she said.

"I better get going before we are late."

I head in the kitchen and packed lunches for my daughter and me. I'm had leftover steak and rice and for my daughter, a Smucker's Uncrustables sandwich. I thought by now she would have outgrown them, but she still liked them. I do too. I'll sneak one behind her back sometimes and blame my wife. To my wife's credit she'll take the blame.

After I packed the lunches, I made a quick two egg breakfast with a couple of slices of bacon. I would make the same for my daughter but she says my eggs suck, so I stopped trying. I took a Jimmy Dean croissant and sausage sandwich out of the freezer. I wrapped it in a paper towel and heated it for about a minute and half for my daughter's breakfast.

I rushed through my breakfast and finished most of it by the time the microwave went off. I got up and checked. It needed about twenty more seconds. I finished the rest of my breakfast, put my dish in the dishwasher and took my daughter's breakfast out of the microwave. I put it on a paper plate for her and popped my head in the hallway.

"I'll wait for you in the car," I shouted.

"Okay Dad," she shouted back.

I grabbed my keys from the bedroom and my wallet from my nightstand. The dog propped her head up. I hugged her head and nuzzled her. My wife walked in and asked me if I was leaving.

I said, "Yes," and gave her a kiss.

"Have a great day," she said.

"You too," I said.

To this day, I appreciate that she tells me that because I was never used to it until I met her. Growing up, my parents would rush me out of the house to get to school. I don't remember them ever saying bye or have a nice day. That may have happened when I was in elementary and maybe middle school but definitely not in high school. I perceived them to be relieved that I was leaving the house for school.

So when my wife and I first moved in together she would say that to me as I was going to class while I was in graduate school. I would just say, "Thanks," and rush out the door. But the more she would tell me that when I left every morning, I really appreciated it and I would tell her to have a great day as well.

I grabbed my lunch, and as a habit, I looked at the dog's bowls to see if she had enough food and water. I noticed her water bowl was low, so I put the lunch bags down on the island and filled her water bowl. I then heard pitter patter on the kitchen floor. My dog then lapped her water.

"Now you get up," I told her. She then took her snout and nuzzled my leg. "I know you appreciate me," I said. I then grabbed our lunches and headed out of the back door and to my garage.

While I waited in the car for my daughter, I checked emails on my phone. Even though I had unsubscribed from a lot of emails, I still had a handful that were useless to me. I did get some notices that some of our bills were ready. I cleared out my emails then turned on the radio. Most of the stations had commercials.

I started to think about my early days of teaching. I had a briefcase full with novels, the class textbook, and a mound of papers that needed grading or that were already graded over the weekend and needed to be returned to students. Over the years, the load reduced. I didn't carry novels and by about my fourth or fifth year, I only had the graded papers. After that, I wasn't bringing anything home.

I had to tell my family members they didn't have to buy me briefcases for my birthday or Father's Day anymore. They were piling up so much that I had to give them to Goodwill. For some reason I thought, "Man, I'm getting old." As I thought that, my daughter opened the car door and sat down. I pressed the garage door opener to close the garage door.

As we made a left toward Orange Avenue, I asked, "What have you got going on in class today?"

"Nothing," she said.

"Did you have homework?"

"Yup," she said as I came to the stop sign ready to turn on Orange Avenue.

"Did you finish?"

"Yup," she said as she simultaneously sent a text on her phone.

"Any tests coming up?"

"Yup."

"Today?" I asked as I made the right turn on to Orange Avenue.

"Nope," she said continuing to text.

I was about to ask her "What's up with these one word answers, but I already knew the answer. She was a typical high school student that wanted to avoid her parents at all costs. I imagined it was probably harder on her since I teach where she attends school. So, instead of correcting her that she should make eye contact with me as I am talking to her and wanting her to be more conversational, I just let it be and found a station that didn't have commercials.

We came to the next stoplight. I looked to my left and saw the antique store. It had the hours painted on the door. Open Wednesday through Sunday, 11-5. Kind of strange to me. I wondered how they made money when it seemed to me that it's hard enough to make money as an antiques dealer. But what do I know. I am not a business major, my degree was in English Lit.

In my twenty years of being in the Cal-Heights area, that shop space had changed four times and they had all failed. I remember the most recent was a vintage clothing store. Next door to that is a barber shop. It's still open but I don't know how? I rarely see anyone go in there. I looked to my right and saw the waitresses from Blackbird Cafe setting up the outdoor chairs and tables. They have the best breakfast in town. Despite its small size, the place is always packed after 8am no matter what day of the week it is.

"It's green."

"What?"

"The light," my daughter said.

"You spoke more than one word. That's a record."

"Oh God," she said as she went back to texting.

CHAPTER THREE

I was about to drive straight to get on the 405, but my daughter told me it would be faster if we turned right. I nodded and made a right turn.

As we were waiting at the light, I thought, "Man, I don't want to go to work." Lately, I had been feeling like that a lot. I wished I could find something else to do. I wished I could retire, but I know I am a long way from that; especially knowing that my daughter was going to college in a couple of years.

Plus, I didn't get much sleep last night. I watched a documentary about Felipe Lopez. He was a Dominican immigrant who moved with his family to New York city and became a high school phenom in basketball. I really connected to the documentary because he was from the Caribbean and it showed his family struggles and how he had made it through to him making it to the NBA.

After the documentary, I was brought to tears because it reminded me of my parents and their immigrant experience. My dad came from Peru with only $40 in his pocket. My stepmom escaped the Cuban revolution. I remember when they were here in California saving up for a house. My dad was working full time and going to school and my stepmom was working full time. They both worked as part time office cleaners two days a week and would bring me along. I would play with my action figures and Hotwheel cars until they finished.

After watching that documentary, I decided to write my parents a letter of gratitude. I must have gotten lost in that letter as I hadn't gone to bed until after three in the morning. The green traffic light brought me back to the present and I got onto the freeway.

My daughter had been right. She had found a quicker route to merge onto the freeway.

I loved and hated the 710. I found it was the fastest route to San Pedro; even when there was construction of the new bridge inside the Ports of Long Beach and Los Angeles. There were rarely traffic problems, but when they happened, they were really bad. You had no chance of getting to work on time if you were going from Long Beach to San Pedro inside the Port.

A lot of it had to do with all the damn trucks that hauled their containers in and out of the Long Beach and San Pedro harbors. You would have a truck crash that held up traffic for a minimum of an hour on average. The other problem was when they would shut down a lane on either the Gerald Desmond Bridge or the Vincent Thomas Bridge for maintenance. One time, someone climbed the Vincent Thomas to the top. We later found out the climber wanted benefits from the Marine Corp that were due to him. Come to find out that this was not the first time he had pulled that stunt.

But when the path was smooth, it was smooth. And today it was smooth, so it lessened the sting of having to go into work.

At night, the drive back over the bridges is even more impressive. During Christmas time you are able to see the very tall cranes that load and unload the containers on to the ships have been decorated like Christmas trees on top. During the day, the same cranes look like steel giraffes sprawled against the background of ships and harbors and containers.

I pulled into the faculty parking lot and parked the car. I know I shouldn't, but I get irritated by the parents who drive to the faculty and staff parking lot to drop off their kids. They know they can get away with it because it's too early for administrators to supervise the traffic and lots. An administrator does not show up until 7:45am. The parents are supposed to go to the top of the hill at the turnabout then come back down and drop off their kids in the front of the school.

There is a sign in the driveway of the faculty and staff lot that says *No Parking. Faculty and Staff Only.* I guessed it's the teacher in me and being a stickler for the rules and wished that some of these parents would not do that. It sends a message to their kids that are sitting in the car with them that it is ok to bend or even ignore the rules. Maybe I am being too anal about it.

As soon as I turn off the car, my daughter reclined the seat backwards. I opened the door and told her I would see her in a little while.

"Okay," she said as she lyed back and closed her eyes. There have been times when, after opening my classroom and heading to the bathroom, I can see my car from the top of the breezeway and I see two or three of her friends in the car talking or sometimes even taking selfies. I find it weird, but that is the way of the world these days.

"Don't be late to homeroom," I told her one last time, as I grabbed my lunch bag from the front seat.

I walked through the parking lot, under the breezeway headed toward the faculty lounge. I saw some students along the way, and we exchanged good mornings. Some of them asked me when our next essay was due. I told them next week and that they needed to do a better job of writing down the due dates in their school planners or check the due dates on my homework page on the school website.

"I never check the website," one of them says.

"That is why you have the grade you have," I said jokingly.

Another student said, "OOOhh, shots fired."

Another student said, "You got roasted, Hahaha."

I walked into the lounge. I was one of the first ones there, so I didn't run into anyone for the first couple of minutes. I checked my mailbox. I saw some junk mail. Most of it was from teaching material companies or teacher resources for novels I was teaching. Some useful, some not. I liked the Novel Units the best. I'd been using them for years. They combine a lot of good activities from SAT prep, to vocabulary and art activities. The buzz word was differentiated learning. The Novel Units have been way ahead of the curve when it comes to having different activities for different types of learners.

I also saw the envelope that had my paycheck. It's only just a stub because I do direct deposit. I keep my stubs in a file for my dad when he does our taxes.

I placed the stub in my back pocket and the junk mail in the trash. The mailboxes intrigue me sometimes because what teachers put in their box. You can always tell the teachers that don't check their boxes much. Those boxes are almost always stuffed so that can hardly fit anything else in their box. It was May, and in one teacher's boxes, I saw a mini Jack Daniels bottle rubber banded together with a small can of Coke. A gift that was given to us by another teacher as a Christmas present. It was still in this individual teacher's box.

Sometimes teachers have prank wars. I remember at a prior school I worked for, a teacher in my department would take half of an eaten bagel, a banana peel and an avocado pit and put it on a paper plate and put it in the mailbox of a friend of his that he would always torture with pranks. This other teacher was no slouch either. He would give it right back. He took a photo of the prankster's dogs and wrote, 'If you see these dogs, they are abused. Please report the owners.' He posted it on the teacher bulletin board.

I walked over to the coffee maker and started the process of making the coffee. I put the filter in the coffee maker and put about ten scoops of coffee and used the water container on top of the maker. The coffee, of course, was either too watery or I put in too much coffee so it tasted like motor oil.

One of the priests said that I need to use 1/3 cup instead of tablespoons. I used to suck at it at first, but I was one of the few teachers who volunteered to even make coffee. I've seen it where teachers leave about a centimeter worth of coffee in the pot with the coffee burner still on rather than turning off the coffee pot or, God forbid, make another pot.

Unfortunately, I've learned over the years teachers can be lazy. Not only do they do this for the coffee, but they leave things around and don't clean up after themselves. It gets so bad sometimes that there have been emails sent by the administration for teachers not to leave dishes in the sink to wash after they use them. It got so bad that an administrator reprimanded the entire faculty during break about not washing dishes and leaving food in the refrigerator past the weekend. Honestly, I've seen things in the fridge for at least a month after grabbing my lunch out of the fridge.

Also, I hate when I see a donut box and I look forward to grabbing a donut and opening the box and the box is empty. What's so hard about throwing the box away if you are the last person to grab a donut? Unfortunately, you would think we are role models all the time, but honestly teachers can be worse than the students.

A couple of teachers showed up, and we greeted each other and one of them started to make photocopies for their class. Early on, I learned it is a mistake to make photocopies in the morning, especially if you are a teacher that does not get to school on time. Back in the day, we were not contractually obligated to show up until 7:45am. Then they changed it to 7:30am. You can always tell the level of experience of a teacher by what time of day they make their copies. The seasoned veterans who are good teachers and don't have a lot of students to tutor after school make their copies after school. The experienced ones get to school right at 7:30 and make their copies. The inexperienced ones, even though they may get to school on time, realize after reviewing their lesson for the day that they need copies and rush to the lounge, but it's too late. There is a line as long as the one at the DMV. The teachers that have it together make copies Friday after school for the entire next week so they don't have to even go near the lounge to make copies. They only thing that they would come to the lounge for is to have some snacks and coffee and to check their mailbox.

After brewing the coffee, I headed to my classroom upstairs. Several students said good morning to me. I told them that as well. I walked up the staircase and opened the door and put the door stop in. I headed toward my desk and turned on my computer. Some students came in to turn in homework. Some wanted me to look over the essay to give them tips and advice. I did that for about 10-15 minutes then checked my email.

There are some general messages about some problems with the dress code and that we need to be diligent about enforcing it.

For the boys - making sure their shirts are tucked in properly.

For the girls - making sure that they're not hiking up their skirts too short.

An in general, making sure that students are not wearing hooded sweatshirts. In the past when it came to hooded sweatshirts, I didn't see the big deal, but there were problems with kids hiding the fact that they were falling asleep. I hated that, especially if you tell them they were asleep and they would say, "I'm just resting my eyes," or if they had their heads down, "but I'm not sleeping."

They could also hide their earbuds and listen to music. But the main reason the hooded sweatshirts became a problem was in the boys bathroom a couple of boys were messing around slap boxing and one of them grabbed the other kid by the hood and swung him around causing the kid to pass out. He temporarily suffocated the kid, so I understand the ban on hooded sweatshirts.

About five minutes after checking my emails, the bell rang. I stood in the doorway checking dress code before the students entered the room. For the most part, it went smoothly, even though I had to tell a couple boys to tuck in their shirts. I warned one boy that if he came to class without a belt, I would have to give him detention. He briefly protested that he didn't have a belt and that the Dean of Students and other teachers know and they don't make a big deal about it. I remind him that I would understand if it were the beginning of the semester, but we are about to end the school year and he knew better, and that I'm not going to put up with any more excuses. "Wear a belt or you can discuss it with the Dean after school." He walked away in disgust.

The second bell rang and I could see straggler students running to avoid being marked tardy by their teachers. Unfortunately, some of these students know they can get away with this because teachers don't enforce the tardy policy.

I walked to the podium in front of the class and the announcements started. First, we start with prayer. After prayer is the flag salute. And after the flag salute, student body representatives make announcements about activities and sports occurring that day. Then at the end, our rector, the head school priest who runs the school, tells his fun fact and joke of the day. My personal favorite is, "Why did the Amish woman divorce her husband? Because he was driving her buggy."

Once all the announcements were done, I went over what we were going to cover for the day. It was an overview of the lesson – a warm up, or bell work to get them started. A quick background lecture on the topic we were covering, some pair work and group work activities, then what's for homework.

It's important to have some type of warm up or the students can get antsy. Once they get antsy, they start to act out. It calms them and settles them in to get ready for class. Plus, the warm up gives me time to take a roll and make sure everyone is in their proper seats. You have to really be on them about the warm up on Mondays and Fridays. On Mondays, most students want to talk about what they did over the weekend. They want to use it as a ploy to waste time to not get anything done in class because it's a regular schedule. Meaning that the class lasts fifty minutes in comparison to a block period where it is, depending on what school you work at, between ninty to one hundred minutes.

A regular day can go quickly without you getting anything accomplished. By the time you get started and take the roll, twenty to thirty minutes have passed. Early in my career, the students had a sense for that time on Monday and Fridays. I would let them talk and discuss their weekend and then by the time I looked at the clock we only had ten minutes left to get through a fifty minute lesson plan.

It was even worse on Fridays, because all they wanted to talk about was what they were going to do over the weekend.

It was a bit of a struggle but I managed to get through the classes without any hitches. I was glad how smoothly everything went considering I was exhausted by the time the third period ended and we went into break. Once the break bell rang, I waited for all the students to exit and I locked the classroom behind and I headed down the stairwell. I felt relieved knowing we were at break but my bubble burst soon after that. I forgot I had break supervision, and the Dean came into the lounge to remind me that I had supervision in the student break area. I hate supervision as it is and to have to do it on a Friday was even worse.

At that moment, I felt like my students do when I go over the homework – they know that there is homework but they hold out hope that I will forget or cancel the homework. But then I go over the homework and then let out a collective, "Ahh man."

Some brave souls will even ask, "Do I *have* to do the homework?" And I always tell them, "No you don't *have* to do the homework or anything in the class. Just like I don't *have* to give you a good grade if you choose not to do the work."

That's exactly how I felt. Ahh man, I really didn't want to do supervision.

These are the times I envy public school teachers. Friends of mine that are public school teachers have told me that the school provides security to supervise the students before, after school break, and lunch. Some of the bigger schools have school police or even the local police come supervise. For us, it's part of our contract because most Catholic schools, especially Archdiocesan schools, do not have the budget to provide security. Plus, I was told my an administrator at one of my previous schools, that having security gives the perception that the school is not safe. and if it's not safe they won't send their kid to our schools, causing enrolment to go down and eventually for the school to shut down. Unfortunately in the last several years, we've struggled and a few area schools had to close.

Plus, each season we even have to supervise at least two after school events, such as a game or activity or school dance. I always avoided school dances. My first year, I got suckered into supervising the prom. Man, was that a mistake. I know back in my day we did the bump and grind, but now they were taking it to another level and it was awkward stepping in and telling them they had to have more distance in their dancing or when they would kiss and have public displays of affection. I didn't even like adults who showed affection in public let alone teens. When they would kiss it looked like a baby horse that was just born, and they wobble awkwardly before they get their footing and start to gallop.

At lunchtime, I walked out to the student area and supervised the far corner of the lunch pad area. I walked around and reminded students to pick up their trash before the bell rang. I have seen some teachers grab a trash can and walk to each table in the area they are supervising and have students throw their trash out. I didn't ever think of doing that. They are not little kids. They needed to know on their own to clean up after themselves.

Some students like to tease me because I am a New York Yankee and New York Giants fan. They like to remind me when they are struggling. I just smile at them and move on.

CHAPTER FOUR

The bell rang, and most of the students moved on quickly, except the seniors of course. I reminded them that classes were about to start, hoping I might have time to enjoy my cup of coffee in peace.

Thank God I don't teach seniors. I taught them one year and that was enough. They're okay the first semester, but then become unbearable little shitheads, especially after spring break. They don't follow the rules, including getting to class on time. Then there are the kids who get accepted early into college and worse, those elite high school athletes who sign their athletic scholarships before the end of the school year. One time I had this kid who was the model student until he signed his football scholarship, and then he turned into a major pain in the ass.

My next two classes went smoothly. When the lunch bell rang, Father asked the students to pray the Angelus prayer and the lunch prayer, and when they finished it was the usual sprint to the lunch line. They leave fast for the lunch break, but it seemed like light speed once that bell rang. I locked up and headed downstairs to the teacher's lounge and found a nice Mexican spread—crunchy beef tacos, chicken tacos, salad, and tamales. Definitely a treat. Some of the parents were caterers and restaurant owners and needed service hours, so they provide lunch for the faculty and staff. I was super hungry and grabbed a bit of everything and joined some of my fellow English Department colleagues.

Maybe I'm sexist, but it's cool to have an all-male staff. At my two previous schools there were always more women than men in the department. It was a nice change of pace. My wife had always told me that women are harder on each other than they are on men. I hadn't seen it in action until I became the assistant coach of the girls softball team. During a playoff game, when the batter hit a blooper in between the shortstop and center fielder, there was a miscommunication and that blooper dropped. It was catchable, but both just stopped and watched it drop. The head coach predicted trouble.

"It's just one play," I said.

He gave me a strange look and told me I hadn't coached girls long enough. The rest of the team wouldn't let go of the missed ball, and the center fielder had tears in her eyes. The tension continued throughout the game, and that dropped ball caused us to lose by one run.

When I taught at an all-girls school for the first time, one of my students pleaded with me to move her seat. When I told her I didn't rearrange the seating charts until the end of the semester and asked what the big deal was, she said she hated the girl that was assigned next to her. I asked what she did that was so horrible? She told me the story, which had happened in the fifth grade.

"Are you serious? That was seven years ago!"

"I still don't like her," she said.

"Well, you gotta tough it out. Sorry."

She walked away all huffy and puffy.

I was baffled. Boys are different, I guess. We can say, "Fuck you," "No, fuck you," and maybe get into a fight, then it's over with. But I've noticed through years of coaching and teaching that many females hold grudges.

When I finally sat down for lunch, the other teachers were talking about TV shows they liked, and I added my two cents worth. The debate got heated when *Game of Thrones* came up. I wasn't really into fantasy scripts and had no desire to watch it. I mean, I did like *Lord of the Rings*, but other than that, I can't do it. Plus, when people overhype a show, I tend to be skeptical. It was sort of like when I was debating in college whether to get a tattoo. In the 1990s, it seemed like everyone and their mother got a tattoo and it just turned me off. I guess I'm an elitist in that way.

Chapter Four

The bell rang before the debate got out of hand and most of us trickled out of the lounge some grabbing extra tacos. Veteran teachers like myself knew we didn't really have to leave until the second bell, even though our principal strongly urged us not to linger. We did it anyway unless she happened to walk into the lounge—then we would get our asses out of there in a hurry. When the second bell rang, I looked to the sky in exasperation and said, "Ugh, do we have to go? I guess it's back to the salt mines." Everyone laughed at that gem I stole from my buddy at a prior school.

But when I stood up, I started feeling kind of strange. Hot all of a sudden. It was a warm day, not sweltering, but my forehead and shoulders were overcome with heat and I started to sweat. I took a couple sips of water to cool down, then headed upstairs before the cleanup bell and the sea of kids that would soon fill the staircases.

I let my students into my classroom, checked the dress code, and took roll, but before I could start the lesson my chest started to get tight and the student projects on the back wall looked hazy and blurred. My breathing got shallow and my chest continued to get tighter and tighter, like I was having a heart attack. I tried to calm down, but the panic kept tightening in my chest. I launched into the lesson warm-up anyway, hoping I could focus and the tightness and shortness of breath would go away. But the feeling that a heart attack was coming didn't stop. So I told my students I needed to step out for a minute. I rushed down the stairs to find someone to cover my class and ran into the Dean of Students and told her I needed to go to the hospital.

I rushed to my car and dialed 911. When I told the operator that I was driving away from the school because I didn't want the emergency vehicles to arrive on campus and freak the students out, my daughter in particular, the dispatcher told me to pull over, so I stopped two streets over and paced up and down the sidewalk until the ambulance got there. On the way to the hospital, the paramedics told me my blood pressure was through the roof, but I was likely not having a heart attack. When they asked why I got into my car and attempted to drive, I told them about a home plate umpire at a Cincinnati Reds game who had grabbed his chest during the game and rushed through a door in the fence behind him, causing a delay of game. No one knew what the holdup was. Reds fans found out later that he'd had a heart attack and passed away on the scene. The umpire's last words to his crew were that he didn't want to alarm the fans.

The paramedic said, "You never should have gotten behind the wheel, Mr. Rivera."

"I didn't want my daughter to find out what happened to me because she is a student at the school."

CHAPTER FIVE

Once I got to the emergency room, a nurse took my information down and admitted me. About thirty minutes later, a doctor came in and took my vitals and told me that there was nothing physically wrong with me. I told him that I had a feeling that's what it was and that it was probably a panic attack and it wasn't the first time it had happened to me. He said that he was going to have a psychiatrist come in and talk to me.

So, there I was; waiting. About forty-five minutes passed, and for some reason, I flashed to 1996 when I got a phone call from my biological mom, Cookie. I say that because she raised me until I was 10. For the rest of my life up to this point, my wonderful step mom raised me. After a while, I called my stepmom "mom" and started to refer to my mother as "my biological mother" or "Cookie" out of disgust.

Around February 1996, I was attending my first year at Long Beach State. I was living with my parents at the time because it was a short commute and cheaper than living in a dorm. At least cheaper for me and not so much for my parents. I had a long break between classes, so I decided to come home and have lunch before going back to class. The phone rang, and I answered.

"Hello," I said.

There was a slight pause. "It's your mother."

I almost blurted what I thought, 'Shit, what does she want now?'

Probably money, even though she knows that I didn't have enough to give her. And even if I did have it, at this point in our lives I wouldn't give it to her.

I especially did not want to talk to her because the last time we spoke, just last week, she gave me a tongue lashing after my grandma died. She called me every name in the book and called me an ungrateful son of a bitch that did not give a shit about her side of the family. She tried to guilt trip me because a month before my grandma was visiting from San Diego, I only spent a couple of hours with her because I headed with a bunch of my friends to a concert that night.

My grandma was bummed, but she was understanding. Cookie though, had it out for me and started yelling that my stepmom and my brothers were not even my family. I was so pissed that I did something that I never thought I would do and that was hang up on her. In a Latino family that is unheard of and taboo because it is viewed as disrespectful. In the Latino world, family is everything. You don't rock the boat even though there is a possibility that your parents or your elders may not be right or worse to disagree with them.

"What's up?"

"You're Uncle Rocco..."

"Yeah?"

"He's dead!" she screamed.

I could hear the phone drop and this loud wail. Then the wail gave into heavy sobbing. I was fucking stunned. I mean, I could understand my grandma dying last week. She had health problems, was seventy-five years old and smoked and drank all the way until she was seventy.

But my uncle...he was forty-three. How the hell did this happen? I just talked to him last week after my Grandma's funeral. This was unbelievable.

Besides being shocked, I was devastated. I remember I was a junior in high school and we were about to play South High school in football. If we won, we would be outright league champs. If we lost we would still be league champs but it would be a three way tie and to me that tainted the league title. We played our asses off. We held them to seven points throughout the whole game but we had trouble scoring and on top of that we missed three field goals. We ended up losing 7-0. I would have rather got blown out than to lose like that.

I remember going to practice the next day and we were all quiet. We were stunned. I remember I couldn't swallow. It felt like someone had died. Up to that point, it had been the most devastating thing I ever experienced. I felt that exact feeling, but now worse because I had loved him so much.

After a while, Cookie kept her composure enough to tell me that she was going to call me back to give me details about the funeral. Two days later, she called. He had lived in Topeka Kansas. He was going to be buried in the family cemetery that was on his in-law's farm. Apparently, after my grandma died, he told his wife that if anything happened to him that he wanted to be buried on their family farm. He said when he visited that the area surrounding the cemetery was one of the most peaceful places he'd ever been, and my uncle was a well-traveled man. He served in the military for twenty years and was stationed all over the world. His two older kids had dual citizenship because they were born in Saudi Arabia when my uncle was stationed there.

Man, I just could not believe it. My uncle had always been a hero to me. He was always there for me. I remember when I was five. I was struggling with the fact that my parents were apart. I mean, I was one years old when my parents divorced. After that, my dad moved to California but still came out to see me once a month and I would overhear him still wanting to get back together with Cookie. But she wouldn't, and I would ask her why. She said she didn't love him, she never did and to leave her alone about it or she was going to slap me.

My uncle, even though he was in the military and and was gone a lot, still made it a point to spend time with me. The most memorable moment was when he would take me to the Turtleback Zoo. We would always visit my favorite bear Monty. To be honest, I don't know if that was the name given to him by the zoo or if my Uncle Rocco give it to him, but I always knew when he was in town that he was going to take me to see Monty and then he would take me to the park next door so I could eat ice cream and play in the playground.

One time he took me, we saw Monty and he took me to the park to have ice cream and play. We were sitting on the bench eating ice cream when we heard this cry for help. There was a tall jungle gym, and a girl was hanging on with one arm. It was a pretty far drop, so if she fell she was definitely going to get hurt. My uncle dropped his ice cream cone and sprinted. I was like where is he going? Next thing I knew, he climbed the jungle gym and caught the girl as she let go. The mother rushed over and thanked my uncle. I thought my uncle saved her life. He is a hero. From that day, I always held him up on a pedestal and took for granted that he would always be around. Now,

I just learned that he's gone. I couldn't believe it. I wanted to cry, but I just couldn't.

But I did later that night. I went out with my buddies and got drunk. I got home and started thinking about this song, by Garth Brooks called *The Dance*. I am by no means a country music fan, but I like this particular song after I watched the video and how Garth Brooks explained why he wrote the song. I grabbed a six pack out of the fridge and sat at the kitchen table and drank and listened to the song over and over as I cried, and after a while my dad came home. I thought he was already home, but he stayed out later than I did.

"Why don't you go to bed?" he said.

So I got up and quietly but stumbling went to bed.

A couple of days later, Cookie told me the details for the funeral. Later that same day, I got a phone call from my Aunt Doris. She lived in San Diego. She suggested that when I book the flight that I should book it for the both of us so we could travel together. At first, I wasn't sure. Just like Cookie, the years of drug use had negatively affected Aunt Doris' ability to make decisions. Naturally it made them flakey and unreliable. But I was in grief and she was family. I reluctantly agreed and had my dad help me book the flight.

Four days later, I got up to head to the airport for my flight. When I got up, I had a bad feeling about Doris. She was supposed to confirm the night before as to when she needed to drive up to meet at my house or the airport. Before my stepmom left, I asked if Doris happened to call but she said she hadn't and I was a little bit worried. I still had hope that she would show up. My dad then asked me if she was coming. I told him that I didn't know. He grabbed some coffee, but I could tell by the look on his face and his body language that he knew it was a waste of time and money booking a flight for Doris. He knew, but I didn't think he wanted to bring himself to tell me after seeing how devastated I was over my Uncle Rocco's death.

I think I held out hope because as flaky and unreliable as she was, when I needed her in a tough spot she was there for me. Growing up with my dad had been tough. He was a disciplinarian. A lot of that had to do with the fact that his dad was even tougher. His dad was the Chief of Police in Peru. So everything was done in military style; very regimented.

As I got closer to high school, I started to resent the way he was raising me. It wasn't until years later that I appreciated what he had done for me and my brothers. But that resentment rose and came to a head when I was in eighth grade.

Chapter Five

Cookie tried to reconnect with me and still wanted me to live with her. I had got into a disagreement with my dad. Honestly, I don't even remember what it was over, but I was pissed off enough to take the offer from Cookie even though in the back of my head I knew that it probably would not be a good idea to move back in with a drug-addicted alcoholic. But I wanted to get away from my dad.

For a little while, it was fun to not have any rules or not be responsible for much. I just had to take care of myself most of the time making meals, showering, keeping clean, and folding the blankets. It didn't bother me for a while that Cookie was selling drugs out of her apartment. She gave me money every chance she could and even convinced me to be a lookout for her to make sure the cops would not bust her. Everything seemed to go well, but there were a couple of bad omens that I didn't pay attention to that would signal that something really bad on the horizon was about to happen.

The first thing was that Cookie felt comfortable to include me in two situations to start. She thought it would be a good idea for her to take me with her to meet with her connection guy. It was an awkward car ride. We went down several different blocks to make sure no cops were following us. As we were circling, I suddenly saw this black guy running naked down the street. I swear, he had one of the biggest dicks I had ever seen, even bigger than the porno guys.

The second was when I asked Cookie if I could go to a concert. She said yes. On the day of the concert, I came back from the store and she had a couple of lines of coke on the mirror all set up.

She said, "Do you want a couple bumps before we go to the concert?"

In my mind I said, 'Hell no. What the hell is wrong with you?' But I just nodded. She even offered to buy me a couple of joints from the weed guy on the third floor.

After that car ride and the concert, I started to feel like things were getting to be a bit fucked up. Maybe I should have stayed with my dad. But it was summertime and I was loving my freedom and independence. I even got my ear pierced; something I know my dad would never in a hundred years would have let me do.

Then there were other signs or omens. I was walking up Bonnie Brae Street, and I saw a guy rip a chain off another guy's neck and start running up the street. I asked my buddy Danny if she saw that. He said no. Then we were in front of our apartment building, The Cameo, and we were talking. Then we heard this loud crash. This lady that was double parked in the street got rear-ended by some Asian guy. The Asian guy was getting out of the car, but the double-parked lady started her car and made a three point turn to go up the street.

She rolled down the passenger side window and I yelled, "Where are you going? You can sue the guy! He hit the shit out of you."

"I gotta go," she said, "I got dope in the car." Then she sped off.

A couple of hours later after that reverse hit and run, there was a knock at the door. Cookie answered it, and it was the guy who ripped the necklace off from earlier..

"Let me get two balloons," he said.

Cookie inspected the chain to make sure it wasn't fake and once she approved, she gave him two balloons. At that moment, it seemed like things were just getting worse but I was still not convinced to go back with my dad.

About a month later, Cookie came home one late Saturday night with this young woman. I was 14 at the time and she didn't look that much older than I was. Cookie decided that she was going to look after her. Ironically, she told the girl (her name was Maria) that she could not do any type of drugs without Cookie being there.

One evening, I went to the park to play some football. I usually was Cookie's lookout in the early evening and night because the Narcs never were around until this time. But on that day, as I was coming back late afternoon from playing in the park, the Narcs showed. Next thing I knew, Cookie was in handcuffs.

She came out and said to me, "Fuckin Maria! She left $3 worth of coke on the mirror on top of the dresser!"

I thought, 'No big deal. She'll be out by tonight or tomorrow at the latest.'

But my Aunt Doris came by to tell me that Cookie had outstanding warrants for her arrest and that she was going to be in jail for at least a month and that she was going to stay with me in the meantime.

For the month that Cookie was there, it was nice having Doris around. She cooked for me and there wasn't the chaos of junkies knocking at different hours and Narcs harassing us. She really looked after me and I appreciated the fact she didn't send me back to my dad. If it were my Grandma Carmen, she definitely would have sent me back.

After a month and a couple of weeks before high school football practice was going to start, Cookie was released from jail. I was happy at first. Then after she was out, she met with her connection.

I came back from the park and she was snorting some heroin with a friend of hers from the fourth floor. When he left, I told her she needed to be careful, that she was going to get hooked again. I didn't understand because a week before she was bragging how glad she was about getting busted because she got sober and now was doing this shit again.

She just turned toward me and said, "Shut the fuck up and mind your own business."

Doris came by later to check on me. I sensed this was the beginning of the end before I would go back with my dad. Which I ended up doing five weeks later. I thanked Doris for everything she had done for me in that month that Cookie was locked up.

When I said that, she looked confused and said, "You're welcome. You're acting like you're going somewhere the way you said thank you."

I didn't tell her, but I knew I was taking the first step toward that realization.

That is a moment Doris always crystallized in my head. That is why I held out hope that she would at least call to tell me in a worst case scenario she was not going to make the flight with me to my uncle's funeral. But there was no call. I decided to give Doris one more shot and called her but no answer. Not even her voice machine picked up. I was disappointed but knew I had to move on to more important things like making the flight for my uncle's service.

My dad dropped me off at the airport. I went to check in with the airlines to get my boarding pass, but I could tell by the look on the agent's face there was a problem. She told me that I could not get on the flight without my aunt because there was some policy about not letting people board a flight if it was booked for two people.

I was pissed off and confused and didn't know what to do. So I called my dad and he came back to the airport to talk to the airlines. The bad news was I could not take this flight, but I could take the next one out and that they would refund us the money for my aunt's ticket. I then called my Uncle's wife, Aunt Wanda, to let her know that I was coming in on a later flight. In the meantime, I went to one of the concession stands and bought a couple of sports magazines. I checked out some of the articles on the college football rankings and some of the stats of the NFL players. While reading, I fell asleep for a bit then heard over the intercom that they were going to start boarding for the next flight to Topeka, Kansas. So I grabbed my bag and headed down the terminal and showed my boarding pass and boarded the plane.

Most of the flight was uneventful except for the beginning of the flight. I saw this attractive brunette woman walking in the aisle smiling at me. I was hoping that she was going to sit next to me but she passed me. Then a very overweight blonde woman approached and she was the one sitting next to me. When we got our food, I finished and tried to take a nap and heard maybe her sister in the seat in front of us asked the overweight lady if she wanted the rest of her meal. I kind of pretended to sleep but peaked to see what the overweight woman would say. She looked to the side of her then in front then behind her and just nodded, and her sister handed her the rest of her meal. I found it strange. Why be embarrassed at this point? If you are hungry, you are hungry.

Once I landed and headed toward the terminal, I was expecting my Aunt Sandy to pick me up, but I didn't see her. Instead, I saw an older white man come up to me and asked me if I was Rocco's nephew?

"Yeah, I am," I said.

"I had a feeling," he said. "You look like him. I thought at first you were his brother."

The older man was Sandy's dad, Earl. He was tall and tan, which surprised me since it was the fall. I loaded my bag and we got in the car. We engaged in a bunch of small talk that I honestly was not really in the mood for. Still, I wanted to be respectful and he was a really nice guy. He asked me a bunch of questions about California and what the weather was like. I told him the weather was nice most of the time. It was the earthquakes you had to be careful of. I felt bad because I could tell I wasn't even present. But I went through the motions and did the best I could and just watched the highway and I was struck by how flat the landscape was but impressed how green it was. It reminded me a bit of Seattle, same overcast weather and just as green but flatter. It took us about an hour to get to the funeral home.

I took one step out of the car and I just had this bad feeling in my stomach. When I turned to close the car behind me, I heard a voice.

"Hector."

I heard feet shuffling quickly toward me and then I got this big hug. It was Cookie. I was really confused. Just a couple of days ago, she treated me like she was going to disown me and now she was treating me like the prodigal son returning home. It was a weird feeling. She took a step back and looked at me, then I noticed her right cheek was really scarred.

"Don't look at my face," she said. "I fucked it up cooking some crack."

I didn't say it out loud, but I thought 'some things never change.' I was embarrassed that she said it. Not because she actually verbalized it, but that she said it in front of Earl.

Chapter Five

Then a woman with light brown hair in her thirties approached me and smiled. She gave me a hug and said, "I'm Sandy, Rocco's wife." For a moment I felt this peace, this relief even though we were at a funeral home. It was a lot different from Cookie, not just in appearance but in demeanor. At first glance, you would have not thought that this was a woman that just lost her husband. She asked how my flight was and if I needed anything to drink or eat. She apologized for her dad if he talked to much on the drive down.

You hear a lot of stories about how people react under adverse conditions. Hemingway was famous for creating characters that showed 'grace under pressure.' You see it at the end of his novel *For Whom the Bell Tolls* when Robert dies heroically and without fear. I was always struck that he saw his circumstances and he accepted them without questioning or blaming. I felt that same admiration the more I talked and the more I looked at Sandy. This was the first time I was meeting her and I already felt like I had known her forever. I felt strange for a second because Sandy was my Uncle's second wife and I hadn't met his first wife yet, even though I knew all about his first wife through family photos and stories from my Grandma Carmen. When I thought that I had this weird feeling like I was betraying his first wife, my first aunt and my cousins, Uncle Rocco's kids. And I feel even more weird now saying Uncle Hector when everyone in his life outside of his life in New Jersey refers to him as Rocco. I don't know if I can call him Uncle Rocco.

Aunt Sandy then introduced me to Carson. Her mother was holding Carson. He looked like he was asleep. Then she introduced me to Carmelita. She looked like she was about seven years old. She clung to Aunt Sandy's leg. I looked at Sandy's face. She had a smile on her face and just kept talking to me but also acknowledged Carmelita by rubbing her shoulders in reassurance. I was a bit envious how attentive Sandy was and how even though Carmelita was clinging on she had a look of comfort and security, something I never experienced at that age.

It was a nice moment but it was quickly fucked up by Cookie's impatience. She put her hand on my forearm and asked me if I wanted to see my uncle. I wanted to just wait. I wasn't ready to go because I was so touched and struck by the moment of affection by Aunt Sandy and Carmelita. I looked at Cookie and nodded.

Then looked at Sandy and said, "Excuse me, I'm going to see Uncle Rocco."

Cookie and I walked away.

CHAPTER SIX

The funeral home was unfortunately small in comparison to other funeral homes I had been in, especially the viewing area that held my uncle's coffin. I saw a couple of people I did not know at the coffin that apparently were paying their respects. The viewing area held about twenty people. I walked toward the coffin, and I was about three feet away from his coffin and I suddenly stopped. It had been years since I had seen him.

    I had been about thirteen at the time. I was spending the weekend with my Grandma Carmen when she lived off of Gaviota Avenue in Long Beach. He was in town for some military convention. We were talking about the Super Bowl and he was sure his Washington Redskins were going to win. They were playing against the then Los Angeles Raiders. He was ultra-confident since The Redskins beat the Raiders earlier in the season. I bet him the Raiders would win because I loved Marcus Allen. So we made a $20 bet. My uncle was smiling ear to ear because he knew in his mind that the Redskins could not lose. I always remembered that smile and how much he looked so much like my Grandma Carmen. A couple of weeks later I got a check in the mail made out to me for $20. But I really remembered his energy. His smile.

    Looking at him now from three feet away, that energy and smile were nowhere to be found. He had a nice suit on but other than that he looked so lifeless so stiff, so lacking in color. I know he's passed on but I couldn't even pretend to go up to that coffin and converse with him. It wasn't him. I couldn't move. I just kept saying to myself, 'I'm not walking up to him. I'm not walking up to him, it's not him, it's not him.'

What made things worse was Cookie walked up to the coffin and kept telling me to come up. I kept shaking my head but she kept pushing.

I finally told her, "Knock it off. I'm not going up there."

Though I was really pissed at her and distraught at the realization that my uncle was gone, I managed to walk out calmly. I just didn't want to embarrass my Aunt Wanda and her family so I was able to find the strength to keep my composure.

I walked outside and stood next to Earl's truck. I looked up at the sky and whispered to my uncle, "I'm sorry, but that is not you in that coffin. I'm not going to remember you that way. I refuse."

I heard heavy footsteps come up behind me and I turned to see who it was; but I already knew. I've heard those footsteps before. Whenever I got out of line as a kid, I heard those footsteps before I would get a slap in the face, the belt, or worse, as when I got older punched in the face. Usually, when I heard those footsteps, I was struck with fear. But this time around, no fear, more like pissed off that she's even coming out with me.

"What the hell is going on?" Cookie said.

"What do you care?"

"I'm your mother."

"Don't make me laugh. You gave that up a long time ago."

"Just remember, I brought you into this world."

"So what? You acted a week ago like I wasn't your son. Now you just want me to be grateful just because you're here?"

"Don't talk to me like that."

"Or what, you're gonna give me a beat down? Give me a break." I walked away from her and toward a fence surrounding a farm that was across the street.

At this point, the sky was dark. Then, I looked up at the sky. Man, I couldn't believe how many stars I could see in the sky out here.

In Los Angeles, you're lucky to see past the smoggy night air and see some constellations. On a really good night, you get impressed that you can even see stars.

This sky was nothing like that. It was as if every single space in the sky was covered by stars. It was like glitter on black construction paper. It was like showing me what's possible in life despite this personal tragedy I was experiencing, like you can find light in the most unlikely of places.

That life did not always have to be dark. It seemed to push away the anger and frustration I felt toward Cookie. Well, at least for a moment because once we got in the car with Aunt Sandy and her family to drive back to her house, Cookie just kept complaining about how quiet it was and how she would never get used to living in a place like this. She needed a lot of lights and sirens and noise to feel like she was home.

I thought, 'Man I wish she would just shut the fuck up.'

Cookie would get beat downs from a lot of her boyfriends and most of the time it was because she would run her mouth until they would get pissed off enough and haul off on her. The only man that didn't hit her was my dad. My Aunt Doris told me a story that once he and Cookie got into a really bad argument, it was so bad that my Grandma Carmen came into the room held Cookie and kept encouraging my dad to slap her to put her in her place but my dad, to his credit, didn't. Knowing my dad, I don't think it ever crossed his mind the way it did with other men that came into her life. I know I am in danger of being disrespectful for saying this, but part of me wished right then that she were a man so I could tell her to shut the fuck up and if she had a problem then I had no issue giving her an ass beating.

I was struck with that thought. It was the second time I felt disgusted with her.

The first time was when I was a sophomore in college. It was a Saturday and my stepmom overheard me making plans to go to a party. She said that first I needed to stick around until 6pm as someone was coming over to visit me. I kind of could tell that it was probably going to be Cookie. I thought about the last time I saw or spoke to her. It was my senior year in high school. I got drunk at a party and thought about her and how she was doing and I teared up because I kept thinking she was going to die alone. I got really sad and miraculously she called the next day.

When I figured out the possibility that it could be Cookie, for a split second, I was looking forward to seeing her. It felt like it was going to be a reunion but all of it changed when she showed up. She looked like shit. She had heavy bags under her eyes. She wore a big dress but it looked like a smock. The dress didn't seem like it was clean. She had on high heels but one of the heels had a big gash going across it. She had a lot of acne. It was pretty bad.

What made things worse was she brought someone with her. His name was Donald. First of all, I was shocked because he was a white guy. Cookie never dated white or even lighter guys. I didn't even know she knew any white people. He had a scraggly rockstar afro that was parted on the side. He had thick ass glasses that had a slight crack in the upper right side lens, and he wore red plaid pants and a beige, plaid sports jacket. He looked straight out of the 1970s.

I looked at her and wondered what the fuck happened. Good, bad or ugly, Cookie always had this energy to her. No matter what, the one thing you can say about Cookie, you knew where you stood with her. When she had something to say, she said it with brutal honesty, but she always brought the energy. That day it seemed that energy was gone and was being zapped from her by being with this guy. She then launched into how the traffic coming from San Diego was horrible and they should have taken the freeway instead of the Pacific Coast Highway. She kept talking but I didn't pay attention to most of what she was saying because I was watching the clock wanting time to move faster so my boys would come over and we could go to this "rager."

Donald and Cookie got up and said goodbye to us. They couldn't get out fast enough. Once they left, my dad went to the living room and turned on the TV. My stepmom looked at me and asked me how I felt about seeing Cookie.

I told her, "I don't know. I thought I would be happier or something."

I couldn't describe it. I always felt like when you see a loved one at the airport, you feel this love and excitement. It was the first time I didn't feel that way when I saw her. Then the doorbell rang and my brother Paul opened the door. It was my boys. They gave fist bumps to my brother and they were on their way to give my stepmom a hug.

But before they did, I looked at her and said, "It was just different this time around."

After I said that and my boys greeted my stepmom and my dad, I was glad that Cookie was gone and especially glad she took Donald with him.

Once we got back to Sandy's and my uncle's house, we ate, drank some beers and shared some stories about my uncle. Then Cookie asked Sandy if she could use her phone. Sandy told her that she could use the phone in the living room because it would be quieter. For some reason, I wondered who she was going to call. I guess this was all strange to me because at that point I didn't really know much about Cookie. I knew that she was living in Puerto Rico, but I didn't know if she was working, collecting welfare or both (which was illegal).

But she did it anyway. When I was in fourth grade, she was collecting welfare and bringing home government cheese while working as a maid at a motel about two blocks from where we lived at the time and getting paid under the table. That is why she didn't get her benefits taken away.

I hated that time period because whenever Cookie overslept, I would answer the phone and it would be her boss Ethel. At the time, I hadn't hit puberty yet. I sounded a bit like Cookie and I would tell Ethel, "I am sorry, I feel a little bit sick, but I'll be there soon," in Cookie's voice.

I had to force Cookie to get up after she went on a bender the night before. I'm surprised Ethel never caught on that I was covering for Cookie and more surprised that Cookie quit and Ethel never fired her for all the times she went in late.

My Grandma Carmen had passed and Cookie wasn't talking to my Aunt Doris, so she was probably going to call one of her boyfriends she had on the Island. I kind of figured that was maybe the case because she seemed giddy when she asked Aunt Sandy to use the phone and she had a bounce in her step when she headed into the living room.

I continued to eat and drink some more and talk with Aunt Sandy and how she met my uncle and how long they had been living in Kansas. Then I heard Cookie calling for me several times. I walked over to see what the hell she wanted.

"Come here," she waved to me.

"What is it?"

"I want you to meet Ramon," she said.

"Who?"

"Ramon, my new man," she said.

"What, am I ten years old? You don't need my approval."

"Just talk to him."

"Why the hell would I want to do that? I'm not looking for another dad. I'm happy with the one I got."

"I just want you to talk to him."

"Why?"

"Because it's important to me."

"It's not important to me," I said and walked back to the kitchen to hang with Sandy and her parents. But before I left I saw the disappointment in Cookie's face. It kind of surprised me because, to be honest, I didn't care or feel guilty about it. As a matter of fact, it felt good to tell her no and to know she had no power over me to convince me to do otherwise. For the first time in my life, I truly felt like I was my own man and making my own decisions.

Aunt Sandy then showed me to my room. I grabbed my bag from the den and walked down the hall, and to my right was one of the guest rooms. It was a nice house but was still stuck in a time warp. The house was right out of the 70s, covered with gold shag carpet and had the fake wood panel walls. I remember my room at my Dad's house had the same paneling. The paneling always tripped me out because you can make patterns with the fake wood. I could see airplanes ships, sometimes Knights of the Round Table. I looked at the paneling, and even though it reminded me of what was at my dad's house, it didn't have the same patterns. I was also super glad that the guest room had its own bathroom. I was done with Cookie for the night and didn't want to hassle with the possibility that I may have to run into her because we would have to share a bathroom.

After washing up, brushing my teeth and all the hygiene stuff that needed to be done, I was exhausted but not sleepy. I was just going through too many emotions to feel sleepy. I thought I would fall asleep easily between the emotions of the morning of missing my flight, the long drive to the funeral home, then to Sandy's house. I thought the jet lag alone would have got me, so I thought for sure I would fall asleep, but I couldn't. I lay and stared at the ceiling, trying to figure out why the hell I was having trouble sleeping.

I suppose it was the human element of all this. Losing my uncle, seeing Cookie for the first time in about six years, and meeting, what felt like a new family, Sandy and her kids, was overwelming. Plus there was the added excitement of knowing that the next day I was about to see my Aunt Barbara, my uncle's first wife, and my cousins Kerry and Rocky, who I haven't seen before other than pictures of them when they were little. On top of that, I was dealing with losing my Grandma Carmen and my Uncle Rocco in the same week.

I thought about how Cookie hammered me that I was a terrible son and grandson because I didn't spend enough time with Grandma Carmen before she got sick and passed. I had a talk with my stepmom about it, and she reassured me that my grandma knew I loved her and that, no matter what, Grandma Carmen loved me. I felt comfort when my stepmom said that because it was true. My grandma adored me. Every time Cookie yelled at me or attempted to discipline me

Grandma Carmen would intervene and defend me. Grandma spoiled me. Whenever the latest toy came out, I would beg her to take me to the store to buy the toy and she would. She would take me to the liquor store down the street from her apartment and she, in her broken English, would tell everyone, "This is my grand charge, this is my grand charge," even after I had met half the neighborhood in that store several times.

Maybe in the moment I was missing her and I wasn't fully aware of it. I mean I didn't have much time to think about things when she died and then *bam!* My uncle is gone. It's a lot of shit that I definitely was not prepared for. Then seeing Cookie after all these years and Doris being a no show. It was hard to make sense of all this shit that seemed to be happening all at once. After about two or three hours, I was able to fall asleep.

I was awakened by the smell of bacon. My Aunt Sandy and her mom were making breakfast for all of us. It was a huge spread – scrambled eggs, pancakes, fruit, bacon, biscuits and gravy, orange juice and coffee. I was starving and had a bit of everything. As I was eating, I noticed Carmelita was staring at me while she was eating. It was so cute and innocent, but I didn't really know what to do. At the time, I was definitely anti-kid. I did not want to have kids, and I definitely did not want to get married. I remember my stepmom asked me when I was going to date a nice girl and hopefully get married. I told her I didn't want to get married, that I wanted to travel the world and have as many affairs as I could with beautiful foreign women. I could tell she was heartbroken.

"Why don't you want to get married?" she said.

I asked her if she saw the remake of the movie Sabrina with Julia Ormond and Harrison Ford. Sabrina asks Harrisons Ford if he was against getting married. He said, *"I'm not married because I believe in marriage."*

"That's how I feel," I said to my stepmom. "The problem is I don't really think I am going to find someone in this day in age, with the high divorce rate, that is not going to see eye to eye with me when it comes to marriage."

She just nodded and said, "It would still be nice if you met a nice girl and started a family."

But seeing how Sandy and my uncle were so happy and how devoted to her kids she was, it at least gave me pause to rethink my views. And seeing little Carmelita's cute little face, I'll admit it warmed my heart a bit when it came to kids. Instead of seeing them as annoying, disease-carrying, booger eaters, I was just so struck at how much she looked like a mini version of my uncle. She then started waving to me and I waved back. I got a sense she noticed when I finished my breakfast. She then came over to the table and grabbed my hand.

"Where are you going sweetheart?" Sandy asked Carmelita.

"To see Christmas Daddy," Carmelita said.

"It's Ok, Hector, you can finish your breakfast."

"It's ok, I'm pretty much finished," I said, "but I will take my coffee with me if that's okay?"

"Sure," Sandy said.

"Besides, how can I say no to a cute face like this?"

Everyone smiled warmly, but I could see the sadness on everyone's face as I walked away.

Carmelita walked me to her room, which had a huge doll house and a bunch of stuffed animals everywhere. Most of her room was pink. I noticed even her TV was pink. I also noticed that the TV was on. Sandy then pointed to the TV.

"Let's watch Christmas Daddy," she said, still holding my hand, then she was guiding me to sit on the floor next to her.

"Ok, " I said looking confused.

I was confused because there was a home video playing on the TV, and every time her dad appeared on the screen she would point and say that her Christmas dad was coming. At first, I thought "What the hell is she talking about? I hope she doesn't have mental issues." I know that's fucked up, but my confusion led me to think that way. Then it all started to make sense to me. The home video was of a family Christmas party, and suddenly my uncle appeared on the screen wearing a Santa hat and hanging gifts out while sipping on eggnog. Everyone was having a great time. Then every once in a while I would look over at Carmelita and notice how much she was smiling, and she silently would just point to her dad like she was communicating directly to him and like he could hear her. I stared and smiled. At the same time I was sad that this was the only way I would see my uncle from here on out. About thirty minutes later, Sandy came into the room and told Carmelita she had to start getting ready for her dad's funeral. When she said that, I gave Carmelita a hug and thanked her for showing me her "Christmas Daddy and that I had a lot of fun watching with her," and I left the room so I could change as well.

I put on my navy blue suit with my navy tie that had red and white tiny dots on it. My dad got it for me a couple of years ago when we attended a friend's daughter's wedding. Well, actually I called him Uncle Carlos. Typically in Latino families, the closest and dearest friends of your parents suddenly become your *Tio's* and *Tia's*. His daughter Caroline was getting married so my dad bought me a suit because I was a poor college kid without a job, so he helped me out.

After we were all dressed, we gathered on the porch and when the porch got full we made our way to the yard. Apparently, we were waiting for a handful of relatives and family friends so we could caravan to the family cemetery. Once those struggling family members and friends showed, we started to pack into the cars. I noticed that Cookie was getting in the car with Sandy, and she started to gesture to me to come sit next to her, and at the same time I noticed Earl getting into his truck with his wife and he had a cab with seats in the back. I looked at Earl and lied to him telling him Aunt Sandy's car is full and asked if I could ride with him, and his wife and he said sure.

It took about thirty minutes to get there, but I really enjoyed the ride. I noticed more cornfields, the fences, and the cattle. Even when we passed farms where I could not see the cattle, I could smell the methane in the air. Earl's wife apologized for the smell. I told her it's not as bad as when I'm on the freeway near Carson and you can smell the Hyperion Treatment Plant. It's a lot worse than methane. What I enjoyed most was not having to hear Cookie complain all the way to the cemetery.

We got to the entrance road of the family farm, drove about a mile then made a left, drove another half a mile, and made another left. There was a fenced area surrounded by cornfields. In some way, it reminded me of the baseball field, in the movie *Field of Dreams* where the baseball field was surrounded by corn instead of a fence, except the cemetery had a fence though there was corn on the other side of the fence that surrounded the whole cemetery except the front. Most everyone parked on the road. Earl almost drove right to the gravesite where my uncle was going to be buried.

We all got out of our cars, and I got out of Earl's truck. I noticed Cookie walking fast toward the casket. Before the funeral started, she stood next to the casket and just let out a huge wailing sound. I never heard anything like that before and I never want to hear it again. For a second, I actually felt empathy for Cookie. I suddenly started flashing over all the moments my Uncle and I had together and I started to get overwhelmed with emotions. It was so bad that I went up to Sandy, hugged her, and said, "I'm going to be next to Earl's truck. I am sorry, but I don't want to see my uncle this way."

About five minutes later, the preacher started to give his sermon. He expressed how much my uncle meant to so many people and shared some personal anecdotes he had about my uncle. Cookie was not wailing, but I could hear and see her sobbing. I then looked over at Sandy, who was standing to Cookie's right side. She was emotional and crying but still had composure enough to put her hand on Cookie's shoulder to comfort her. As that happened, I walked on the other side of Earl's truck so no one could see me, and I got on one knee and just lost it.

Honestly, I don't think I have ever cried like that in my life. The closest was a year before, when one of my good friends was shot in the back. The family asked me to be a pallbearer at his funeral. I did not feel any emotions through the funeral until his casket was being lowered into the grave, and I just lost it. At that time, it was the hardest moment I had ever experienced but this now, with my uncle, was on another level and I didn't know how I was going to react if I watched my Uncle's casket being lowered into the ground. I just couldn't bring myself to witness it, and I felt guilty about it because in a way, I felt like a coward that I didn't go stand next to Sandy and not be there for the sermon and the lowering of the casket. As I was on my knees and suffering behind that truck, I heard a cow rustling in the corn and the moaning of a calf following behind her. When I heard that, I somehow calmed down. And then I felt a hand on my shoulder. I looked up, and it was Sandy. I cried even more because I wished I could have been as brave as she was.

After that, pretty much the whole rest of the day was a blur. I remember we drove back in the direction of Sandy's house. Just before we got there, we made a turn on one of the roads and then we drove up to a VFW. That is where they were having the reception. I noticed some people gathering around Earl's truck. They were thrusting their hands and introducing themselves. They expressed their condolences and how great a guy my uncle was, and they were struck that I looked so much like him. Some of them even thought Uncle Rocco was my brother. I was flattered by that, but I was still in shock that he was actually gone. And so soon. I didn't understand it. When my dad's father died, it made sense to me. He had health problems for years. Toward the end of his life, he had to have dialysis, and he was diabetic, but he lived to be 75. Grandma Carmen too. She was 77 and was still drinking whisky and smoking cigarettes. But my uncle . . . it just didn't make any fuckin sense to me.

Some of my relatives I talked to on Cookie's side of the family believed in spirituality a lot and they believed my Grandma Carmen took my Uncle Rocco with her. I can be superstitious about sports but that is the extent of it, but I believed my relatives, it made sense to me that my Grandma took him with her. They were very close, so I could understand it but why now when he was only 43 years old. It felt so unfair because he's my uncle, unfair because he was so young, unfair because he had an awesome wife, unfair because my cousins are going to grow up without their father.

I don't remember much about the reception other than greeting a lot of people and eating a lot of food. Then we headed back to Sandy's house, where the atmosphere was very somber. Even Carmelita was playing quietly in her room. Sandy was putting Carson to sleep, and Cookie was out on the porch smoking a cigarette. I could see her body language, and even though I couldn't see her eyes I could see the sadness and depression in her profile. She would inhale, exhale, flick her cigarette, and sit there cross-legged. Something definitely was on her mind. I remember seeing her in this state as a kid, nothing good came of it. I remember the first time I saw her like this I was five. After chain smoking a couple of cigarettes, she came into the living room to tell me she was going out. Hours later, she came stumbling in, and you could smell the fact that she had been at a bar. The good thing was she didn't bring a man home. She then dragged a kitchen chair by the window and clumsily took out a cigarette, and dropped her pack as she was lighting the cigarette. I picked up the pack for her.

She then started smoking her cigarette and she looked the same way she did now, and asked me, "Do you know what today is?"

"No," I said.

"Today would have been your grandfather's birthday," she said.

I asked her where he was because she had never ever brought him up before. She took another puff of the cigarette. She told me that he died. She told me some faint memories she had of him. She found his body on the bathroom floor. He basically drank himself to death and was convinced that my Grandma Carmen drove him to it. She also said that Juan, his name, was the only good man, besides my Uncle Rocco, that she had ever known. I didn't know what to say, but the sad part was that this image of her near a window or on a fire escape was not the last. The stories and her benders always got worse. Besides alcohol, she graduated to hard drugs, cocaine and heroin. She would wait until I was asleep then take some bumps thinking I was asleep. She even snorted the heroine because I never witnessed her shoot it up.

She later told me on one of her alcohol-drug benders that the reason she did that shit in the first place was that she got hit by a car when she was 10 and has been in pain ever since.

At that moment, she had that look like she wanted to go on a bender. I wasn't about to go on that porch for her to share another tragedy to justify her actions and behavior. I just didn't have the patience and energy to do it, but I was curious about what she was going to do. I remember watching a reality show about celebrities in rehab. The show documented the celebrities taking their last "hits" before admitting themselves. I remember this one beautiful supermodel that was about to go on a photo shoot. I don't quite remember the drug, but it was definitely a pill. It might have been ecstasy, and she looked at the camera and said that the pill, "was to scratch that little itch on the edge of her brain." I remember that look on the supermodel's face. She was so pretty, but there was this edginess, a need to be free of something, and that pill was going to set her free. Cookie had that look like she wanted to be set free.

The longer I watched her, I felt a gleam of hope, optimism that she wasn't going to give in to that urge to set herself free through chemicals. The thought kind of surprised me because I was still pissed off and frustrated with her for the shit she said about me and my dad's family when Grandma Carmen had her stroke. I heard some shuffling coming from the kitchen, so I turned around to pretend that I was still watching TV instead of Cookie. It was Sandy. She gave me a hug and told me good night and if I was still hungry that there was some extra food in the fridge. As she was about to leave the room, she looked at me and thanked me for spending time with Carmelita. She then smiled and said, "Your uncle was very proud of you, and he loved you very much." I could see her face quiver a bit, and I noticed her getting teary eyes and when she saw that I noticed she quickly but quietly left the room.

I got a little choked up, but my emotions were interrupted by the thought of Cookie on the porch with that look like her skin was starting to crawl. I looked back out of the window. She was about to finish her cigarette but gave a couple of flicks before her last puff. She took her last puff then put out the cigarette with the heel of her shoe and dropped it in the coffee can next to the chair. She got up and looked into the kitchen window, probably to see if Wanda was still in the kitchen. She then started walking toward the living room window where I was. I leapt off the couch and hid in the threshold of the door separating the hallways that led to the bedroom from the living room.

Chapter Six

I waited there and could hear faint footsteps on the porch and knew she was away from the window.

I quietly made my way back to the living room and looked out to the porch to see where she was. She stood on the top step of the porch stairs, staring straight ahead like she was staring into nothingness. She still had that look like she needed that itch on the edge of her brain to be scratched. She just stared with her hands in her pockets, like she was waiting for permission for something. I looked back at the clock behind me, and only five minutes had passed, but it seemed like she was standing in that position forever. It reminded me of that final shot in the John Wayne movie "The Searchers" where there is a shot from inside the cabin of John Wayne with his back to the cabin walking away. It's such an iconic shot but it's iconic for me because it seemed there was just such a finality to it, like you were passing into another world. I was seeing the same thing, but it was from the side of Cookie rather than from behind.

I honestly don't know why I sat there and watched her other than it was a very mysterious moment, and I've always been attracted to mystery even though they were moments I knew better. But there I was looking and wondering. What the hell? Make a decision already. She took a couple of steps back like she was going back into the house, but she suddenly paused. She still had her hands in her pocket. Her head slumped. I then saw tears stream down her face. She had the same body language and tears she had when she was near my uncle's casket that afternoon but without the wailing and flailing of her arms and body. She turned back around and walked back to the top step of the stairs of the porch with her hands still in her pocket and her head still slumped. She then looked up to the sky for a while like she was looking for an answer.

Finally, she stopped looking at the sky and looked forward. Instead of confusion or wanting to scratch that itch in her brain, she had a look of laser focus, of determination. She was now standing erect, back straight. She then took her hands out of her pocket, took a deep breath, then reached down in her jeans in her crotch area to pull something out, and once she pulled it out she walked off the porch and toward the shed that was to the left side of the house and she disappeared behind the shed. I turned around to watch TV feeling disgusted. Then I decided to turn off the TV and muttered under my breath, "I fucking had a feeling," and I walked toward the guest room to get ready to go to sleep, especially since my flight was leaving in the morning.

The next day, my flight was going to leave before my mother's flight. I went into the other guest room where Cookie was sleeping. For some strange reason, I felt obligated to say goodbye to her, but more out of respect for my Uncle and Wanda, but she was asleep. I stood in the doorway looking at her. I was still thinking about the evil things she said to me and about my dad's family and the fact that she gave into that scratch during my uncle's funeral and at Aunt Sandy's house. I wish she would have just gone off the property or gone to a local bar to do that shit. I thought about how distant I had become from her. For a moment, I suddenly felt sorry for her, and I felt scared that she was going to die alone, and said to myself, this may be the last time I see her. And I was ok with it for some reason, I just knew that if she passed, that I definitely won't wail for her the way she did for my uncle.

I grabbed my bag and headed to the living room. Carmelita and Carson were still asleep and Earl was in the kitchen grabbing some coffee. He asked me if I would like a cup.

I told him, "No thanks."

Then he asked me if I was ready to go and I nodded that I was. As I nodded, Carmelita was standing in the kitchen doorway made her way toward me.

"It was so nice to finally meet you," she said.

"You too," I said, "Thank you for everything."

"Of course, You're family."

"Give hugs and kisses to the kids for me, and tell your mom I said bye."

"I sure will," she said.

Earl started walking out the door, then I turned to follow and heard, "Hold on one sec," from Aunt Sandy.

Earl then said, "I'll take your bag," and he left the front door to go to his truck. I heard footsteps coming from the bedroom, then the hallway, and Sandy emerged. She then slowed her trotting to a walk, grabbed my hand, and put something in it then clasped it closed with her hand over the top of mine. I smiled at her then opened my hand to see what it was. It was my uncle's military dog tags. I got choked up but did not want to cry so I could look at the tags. It had his full name. Rumor was that his middle name was after his father, but I heard from some reliable relatives that Grandma Carmen really did not know who Uncle Rocco's real father was, that she just named him after the man she last had a relationship before he was born, which I found strange because both Cookie and Doris told me that Juan

Chapter Six

had caught Carmen cheating with another man in their bed, and he stabbed the both of them. Then I looked, and it said his birthday and his religion, Roman Catholic. I just stared at the tags in awe.

"I don't know what to say . . . just thank you and I shouldn't take this," I said.

"Yes, you should," she said.

"What about Carmelita and Carson and Uncle Rocco's other kids? They should have them."

"They will have plenty of things from their dad."

"I just don't feel right, I feel like I don't deserve them."

"Yes, you do. He would share stories with me about how he used to take you to the zoo to see your favorite bear Monty when he was on leave. He said that when he would look at his dog tags that it reminded him of all those times you went to the zoo."

I suddenly was overwhelmed and started to cry, and she hugged me and said that I definitely deserved the tags. After I calmed down, she gave me one more big hug, and I walked off the porch and headed toward Earl's truck where he was sitting in it and the truck running. As I got in the truck, for some reason I looked at the shed and then I quickly got into the truck. The drive to the airport was pretty quiet as I held my uncle's dog tags and just kept staring at them like a valuable relic that I had not seen before. I could tell at times that Earl wanted to talk and out of the corner of my eye I could see him turn his head toward me but tears just kept flowing and I didn't care if Earl saw me crying or what he thought, I just kept crying the more I looked at the tags because so many memories of me and my uncle just kept flooding me.

A week later, I got back into my routine. I had late classes so I was able to sleep in a bit. I liked it because my younger brothers went to school and my parents were at work so I loved the quietness and I could make breakfast for myself in peace. I turned on the TV for a bit. And of course there was nothing good to watch – nothing but soap operas and talk shows and news shows on the regular channels and a bunch of movies or TV shows or reruns on the cable shows. I remember when we first had cable there were maybe 20 channels. Now there was like a little over a hundred. I think the cable station did this so a viewer can find something to watch, but as one person put it, we now have over a hundred channels of not finding something to watch, so I turned to old reliable, ESPN, 24-hour sports. Even though I had it on, it was more like I was using it for background noise as I was eating breakfast.

After that, I headed upstairs to get ready. After I got ready, I grabbed my backpack, my keys and headed downstairs to go to class. I bent down to pet our dog, a white fluffy Maltese, and said, "See you later," and went out the front door toward my truck. As I was about to get into my truck, I noticed our neighbor Elizabeth from across the street watering her lawn and of course she was staring at me as I was getting in my truck. I couldn't stand that bitch and wanted to yell out, "What the fuck you lookin at," but knew she would probably call the cops and have me arrested for assault.

When we first moved into this house on the cul de sac, my Samoan homeboys helped out. After we got all our stuff into the house, Elizabeth walked over and was having a conversation with my parents. As I went back to the U-Haul for the last couple of things I heard that bitch say, "It's usually quiet around here until today. Hopefully, it will remain that way." Then our Maltese came charging out and barked at her. She then looked at our dog and said, "She must not like white people."

My dad turned around and said, "What are you talking about, the dog is white?" and I laughed in that bitch's face when my dad said that.

I got in my truck and headed off to my classes. As I drove off, I stared at her and mouthed "Bye bitch," under my breath. I then made a right, then another right, then another left on Del Amo Boulevard and then made a right on Anza, then right on 190th and then took that to the 405 and took the 405 South to Bellflower Boulevard. I then made a left on Atherton, and before I got to the pyramid structure, I made a right into the huge Cal State University Long Beach parking lot and then head to the parking structure nearest to the building next to my three classes I have for that day.

I got to class, but most of the day was uneventful other than I kept thinking about what happened over the weekend of my uncle's funeral. It was a lot to take in honestly. Once I was done with classes, I got in my truck and got back on the 405 north and headed back home. Just around the Torrance area near the Crenshaw freeway exit, I started to feel weird. My heart started racing. I started sweating, I could feel my heart beating so hard I felt like it was going to claw its way out of my chest. Then I started experiencing shortness of breath. I literally felt like I was going to die.

I got off on Crenshaw and made a left into a Denny's parking lot. My heart was still beating really fast, so I just closed my eyes

Chapter Six

and honestly waited to die. I asked God, "Please don't let me die." I kept my eyes closed and noticed that my heart was slowing and that my breathing was back to normal. I slowly opened my eyes and just looked forward and saw seagulls fighting over a bag of Cheetos in the parking lot. I paid attention to the first conscious thought in my head, and that thought was to call my stepmom. I continued to drive home, and once I got there I called and told her what happened to me.

I said, "I think I need help."

And she calmly said, "Ok...we'll get you help."

But I understood that she was probably shocked that I threw this on her all of a sudden.

I got off the phone and just sat at the dining room table trying to figure out what the hell just happened. I was confused as hell. I then got up from the dining room table and went upstairs to my room to grab the University Catalog. I remember seeing an advertisement on a shuttle bus on campus about if you are struggling you are not alone and you should come to the health center. I talked to the nurse, and she recommended I talk to the Psychology Department. The department offered free therapeutic services. I called and talked to the department secretary and set up an appointment to see a therapist in a couple of days.

I decided to call one of my closest buddies and I told him what happened. Then I told him that I called the Psych Department at school and that I had an appointment in a couple of days.

"That's great," he said, "but you probably don't really want to go to a therapist at your school."

"Why not?"

"They'll most likely match you up with a grad student trying to get units and hours for their degree license."

"Then what the hell do I do?"

"Listen . . . let me give you my therapist's number. She's great."

"You see a therapist?"

"Yeah, why?"

"You seem like you don't have problems," I said.

"I have plenty of issues' I just learned to work through them."

"Man, really?"

"Yeah," he said. "I've been going for about three years. She does excellent work. You're going to have to pay for it, but believe me it will be money well spent."

"I appreciate that," I said.

"Here is her number. I would give her a call ASAP."

"Cool. Yeah, I'll give her a call."

As soon as I got off the phone with my buddy, I dialed the number and waited for her to answer but no answer. I got her voicemail instead. Her name was Dr. Westfield and requested that I leave my name, number and a brief message so I did. That was the first time I experienced a panic attack.

CHAPTER SEVEN

My thoughts and reflections were then interrupted by a nurse that came to check my vitals.

"The doctor will be in shortly," she said.

"How much longer?"

"Soon."

"It's been over an hour."

"He'll be in to see you."

"When?"

"Soon." She smiled and left my room.

I felt so lost and frustrated. Especially since I was sitting in a hospital wearing a smock when apparently nothing was wrong with me physically. I knew why I was in here. So, I just wanted to hurry up and hear what the doctor had to say and be released, and as soon as I said that, the psychiatrist walked in.

"How are you doing, William?"

"Hector, please. When I hear William I look behind me and look for my dad."

"No, problem Hector," he said.

"So tell me what's going on?"

"I had a panic attack," I said.

"It seems that way. Nothing is wrong with you physically," he said.

"I'm just confused by it," I said.

"Why is that?"

"This is the third time this happened," I said. "The two other times, I knew exactly what caused them, but this time around, I have no idea.

"That's ok, what is important is you were able to calm down and you're a healthy guy, so physically you have nothing to worry about, but I am concerned that this is the third time," he said as he scribbled down some notes. Plus, you had to call 911, that is my biggest concern that this was something you had trouble coping with."

"Yeah," I said, "but at least I know there is nothing wrong with me physically."

"Yes, that's true."

"If you don't mind, I just want to ask you questions related to family history."

"That's fine."

"Are you on any medications?"

"Just for cholesterol."

"What are you taking?"

"Lipitor," I said.

"How long have you been on it?" "Fifteen years, probably."

"Any family history of illness?

"My biological mother was bipolar," I said. "Back then it was called manic depression, but I've been told it's the same thing."

"Any family members die by suicide?" "No but my biological mother attempted it."

"Do any family members have substance abuse problems?"

"My biological mother, my aunt, and other cousins on my mother's side and my uncle on my father's side."

"That I know of, just my biological mother."

"Any family members with dementia?"

"Some members of my mother's side died of Alzheimer's."

"Are you a worrier?"

"I tend to be," I said.

"Do you maybe worry about a couple of things, or do you worry about everything?"

"I sometimes worry about everything," I said.

"For how long?"

"Not sure," I said. "There are times I worry about a couple of things and there are times I'm constantly worried. When I feel high levels of stress I worry about everything."

Chapter Seven

"Can you handle it when you're worried or do you feel like it paralyzes you?"

"It only paralyzes me when I have have panic attacks."

"Do you feel like your panic attacks are frequent?"

"No," I said.

The doctor finished his questions then wrote notes on his clipboard. He then took a few minutes to look over his notes. The suspense of waiting for what he had to say was killing me., especially after watching his body language and his facial expressions. I couldn't really tell what he was going to say, but it seemed serious, and it didn't seem positive of what he was going to say after he looked over his notes. Before he spoke, he kind of crossed his arms with his clipboard.

"The good news is that there is nothing physically wrong with you. And I don't see that you want to hurt yourself, and you don't want to hurt others."

"But?"

"But one of the things that bothers me is, are you disabled by this."

"I'm not," I quickly answered.

When I answered the psychiatrist sighed. "It's my recommendation that you get further evaluated, especially that this is not the first time that this has happened to you. I think that you should volunteer for a 72-hour hold at a mental care facility."

"A psych ward?"

"I wouldn't quite call it that," he said.

"I would."

"It's just a recommendation. Let me go back to my office and record my assessment and I'll be back. It will at least give you some time to think about it."

"Fine," I said, and the psychiatrist left my room.

CHAPTER EIGHT

Friday morning, I looked at my desk and saw the phone number of Dr. Westfield written down on a piece of paper. For some reason, I felt fine, like I didn't need to see the therapist, so I picked up the phone and left a message canceling the appointment.

After the weekend passed, I went through my usual routine then got in my truck and headed off to my classes. I went a little early so I could study for an exam I had that day. I walked toward the library and saw a flier on a kiosk that was about study abroad in England. Being an English major, this of course made sense. 'How cool would it be to study in England?' The meeting was going to be after my first class, which was perfect because my next class was not going to be for another hour after the first class, and according to the flier, the meeting was not going to take more than thirty minutes.

I went to the auditorium classroom where they were going to have the meeting. I sat down with the meeting about to start in another ten minutes. I grabbed my short story collection for my short story class and read the story that we were assigned called *Volk Tech* by Theodore Weesner. I read a couple of pages and then my heart started racing, and I felt the sweats. I realized that I was experiencing the same shit as when I was in my truck on the freeway on my way home from class. What seemed to trigger it was that I started to think about this study abroad program more in detail. I was excited at first but then thought, 'How am I going to pay for the plane ticket?" Even though I may have a place to stay, am I going to have to pay for any type of room and board? What about if I have to travel? My mind was spinning out of control. As soon as I saw a person walking up to the mike ready to introduce themselves and the program, I high-tailed it out of there and went to the campus cafe to get something to drink.

After classes, I headed home. I started thinking about what happened to me in that auditorium classroom. At first, I couldn't make heads or tails of it, but I suddenly felt ashamed and embarrassed. Why did I have such a strong reaction to something that was positive? This was a once in a life time experience, and suddenly I felt like I was being tortured like I was suffering. Then to run out of there the way I did, I just felt like a coward, like my uncle was looking down on me and was embarrassed.

Late that evening, I decided to call my buddy and tell him what happened. It told him that I felt like this may never stop.

"You should make another appointment," he said.

"She probably won't see me now since I flaked on her."

"It's not like that," he said. "You're just embarrassed by the study abroad situation and canceling the appointment."

"Well, yeah."

"You have nothing to be ashamed of. Dr. Westfield will understand."

"How do you know?"

"Number one, she gets paid to listen to people's problems. Plus, you're my friend, so she's not going to bail on you. Even if you weren't my friend, I don't think she'd bail on you for canceling an appointment."

"You sure?"

"Yeah." He paused for a moment. "I'm gonna tell you something, but don't tell anyone ok?"

"I won't."

"I don't know if you knew, but I'm the youngest brother. I had a brother besides my oldest brother."

"You did?"

"Yeah . . . and we were really close..."

"You don't have to talk about it if you don't want to."

"Nah, it's all good," he said. "We were close, then we drifted. When we were in high school, he started gang banging. Two years later, he was murdered. I was fucked for a while. I was going out to the clubs and bars pissed off, I drank and drank and would start bar fights. Then I stopped going out and locked myself in my room. I only

Chapter Eight

left to go to work. My ex-girlfriend noticed a change in me, so she gave me Dr. Westfield's number. She knew I needed help. She and her family had been seeing her."

"Wow, that's heavy," I said and paused. I took in what he just said and thought about the parallels between his brother and Cookie. Being close at first, then trying to help that person, then drifting apart.

"I canceled my first appointment," he said.

"You did?"

"Yeah, I canceled five times."

"Seriously?"

"Yup. So you have nothing to worry about. You just have to do the work. Look, if you don't learn to deal with this you'll just keep running. And I don't see you as a runner. Look, I gotta get goin…just call her."

"I'll think about it."

"Don't think, do."

After I ate dinner, I went upstairs and started reading and studying. It was difficult for me to concentrate. I thought about what me and my buddy talked about and how he said I should just call. I fucked up today by leaving that study abroad meeting, but my buddy was right, normally I am not a runner. I knew that if I didn't do something I could end up like Cookie just living desperately, hanging on by a thread, and I didn't want that for myself. So I picked up the paper with Dr. Westfield's number on it, and left a message apologizing and saying that I would like to meet with her any day she could see me.

CHAPTER NINE

My reflection was temporarily broken when out of the corner of my eye I saw a doctor walk by, and when I looked up I realized that it wasn't the psychiatrist that was treating me. I had earlier called my wife and told her what was going on, and I made her promise that she would not tell our daughter what was going on. My poor wife. This was the second time that I put her through this, but thank God she did not have to witness this firsthand. I remember when we first dated, I had told her stories about Cookie. At first, she admitted later, she thought I was making up these stories in order to get her to date me, then she met Doris and other members of my family from Cookie's side when we went to Jersey during our honeymoon and heard the stories repeated from other family members.

I looked up at the clock. It was about 5:15pm. I wanted to get the hell out of there already.

I thought about my first session with Dr. Westfield. I got in my truck and on the 405 and headed toward Long Beach. Dr. Westfield's office wasn't too far from my school campus. Even if I would have had classes, it still would have worked out. I got to her office a little earlier than expected, so I parked and just chilled listening to music. About ten minutes before my appointment, my heart started racing again. I suddenly wanted to cancel my appointment again. I honestly didn't know what to do. I wanted to run like hell again. I turned on my car and put it in drive. I made a right turn and came to a stop sign. I turned my left signal and thought about my dad; he was in my head telling me to turn around. I turned my right turn signal on and circled around the block and parked my car in the same exact spot. I waited five more minutes while thinking about the conversation I had with my buddy then thinking about my dad. I thought about lately, probably since high school, my dad and I had not connected very much. As a matter of fact, we've barely spoken to each other even though we live under the same roof. The only thing we do is be cordial to one another but no conversations, but he does find things to complain about. I think I just stopped trying after I completed my Associate of Arts.

At the dining room table, he and I went through a stack of applications of colleges I was interested in. He went to the fridge and took out some leftovers, put it on a plate and warmed it in the microwave. He looked at me going through the stacks. When his plate was warmed up, he grabbed a fork and knife from the drawer, looked at me and said, "Not sure you're going to get into those places with your GPA," and walked away. I was so devastated that night, I cried myself to sleep. Can you believe that, a grown man crying over a college decision. I should have been pissed, I wanted to be pissed, but I just buried my head in the pillow and cried. I never told my dad I did that.

I got out of my truck and headed to Dr. Westfield's office. There was a Cajun restaurant across the street. There was a staircase leading up to her office. I walked up the staircase then there was a green door with a doorbell. I rang the doorbell. Then seconds later there was a voice that said, "When the door buzzes, turn the knob and push." I heard the buzz and entered the green door. There was a lobby with two chairs. Behind the two chairs were three bookshelves filled with self-help books. I then saw an orange book. I forgot the title of the book, but it suggested you write all your feelings down, especially if they were negative feelings, and you go to a safe place and you burn those pages and it is supposed to make you feel better. I was hoping the therapist didn't want me to do that because I was afraid I could potentially turn into an arsonist.

In front of me and the chairs was a glass window and a glass door, and to the left of the room was a floral patterned couch. It was very clean but looked like something from the 1980s, like it could be part of the movie *Ferris Bueller's Day Off*. Then to the right of the room was a staircase. I continued to look around the room. I didn't see anyone behind the glass window. I found it creepy that you could see

Chapter Nine

the entire room completely but no one was there. It reminded me of a psychology experiment where you are behind a glass partition and the psychologist conducting the experiment only comes in to check on you and makes notes on their clipboard then leaves the room for you to be by yourself. That's the feeling I had.

I suddenly didn't want to be there. Did I make a mistake setting up this appointment? I knew I needed help, but I wanted to get up and leave. A couple of minutes later, I did get up and pace back and forth a little bit and kept looking at the green door several times. One of the times during my pacing I walked up to the green door and actually put my hand on the knob. I was ready to turn it and for some strange reason, I thought about my dad again.

I let go of the knob and at that moment I heard a door behind me open and someone say, "Are you Hector?"

I turned around and there was a lady who looked like she was in her mid to late fifties with spiky gray hair and snake skin heels.

"That's me," I said.

"Come on in," she gestured to me.

She waited until I entered, and I was in the middle of the room. She closed the door behind me. I looked to my left ready to sit on the floral patterned sofa. She said, "Hi I'm Dr. Westfield," and I looked to my right and she was holding out her hand. I reached out and shook it. "Welcome," she said. Then she asked me to follow her. She walked to the staircase and walked up and I followed behind her.

I looked at the walls. I felt like I was in a time warp, like I was back in the 1980s with the color scheme and some of the portraits of ships and seascapes that were popular back then. We made our way to the top and there were two loveseats facing each other, and she asked me to sit on the blue one and she sat on the green one. As I was about to sit down, I saw a small table on the right of the blue loveseat. On the table sat a box of tissues. I wondered what those were for.

After I sat down, she asked me what brought me in. I told her about my trip to my uncle's funeral and when I had a bunch of flashbacks and emotions that caused me to have a nervous breakdown. I told her specifics of what went through my mind and most of it was shit that happened to me as a kid living with Cookie. It felt good letting all of that off my chest, and it felt good because I never experienced someone who was sitting there listening. I mean you do have close friends and family that listen but after a while, they feel the need to put in their two cents when you haven't even finished saying what you have to say, and you feel judged and then regret like maybe you shouldn't have said anything.

When I felt finished, my therapist then asked me what I was feeling? I sat and thought about the question for the moment.

"Feeling?"

"As you are sharing these experiences, what are you feeling? What I mean is, at this moment, what are you feeling?"

"I...I'm not sure. I don't feel anything," I said.

What I was feeling was frustration. I didn't know what I was feeling, or what to say at the moment. Then, I was embarrassed. I was going to tell her that, but I heard a mini-alarm go off, then she pressed on a button on a small clock she had on her table next to her love sofa.

"Well, it gives you something to think about next week," she said.

"Next week?"

"I assume you would like to come back," she said.

"You think I should come back?"

"I think it would be wise," she said. "But it's your choice."

"Can I think about it and I will call you on Monday?"

"Sure, no problem," she said.

I shook her hand and walked down the staircase, exiting the glass door. I saw a woman sitting on a seat in the lobby. We exchanged smiles, then I exited the green door, went down the other staircase and headed to my truck. I thought about whether or not to come back as I sat in the driver seat of my truck. It felt good to get that off my chest and not feel judged or ridiculed. I just didn't know she wanted me back that soon, but I did feel I had more to get off my chest, so yeah, I did want to come back. I knew in the back of my mind I need to come back, especially having that talk with my buddy after he revealed to me the death of his brother.

I was leaning toward coming back next week. I turned on my truck and headed toward the freeway. As I got on the freeway, I thought about my dad again. Part of me was confused because why didn't I bring up my dad in my therapy session when that was the first thing I thought about before I entered Dr. Westfield's office for my visit.

This time thinking about my dad was different. I thought back about two years prior to when my grandfather died. I remember getting a call from my dad. He was the type of guy at that point in our relationship where he did not show a lot of emotion, but hearing him on the phone I could tell he was worried about something. He asked me if I could go to my grandparents apartment because my grandpa had fallen down. I had class in an hour but I felt obligated.

I always felt obligated to my grandparents because of my dad being the dutiful son. When I was in middle school, my grandmother called my dad to tell him my grandfather was having health problems in Peru. My dad realized that he would get better health care here in the States. So, he decided to move both of my grandparents here. It was a struggle with them living in our house. I thought my dad was a tough disciplinarian, but Grandpa was worse. We (my brothers and I) were used to going in the kitchen and getting snacks. Grandpa did not like it and forbade us from going into the kitchen. I lived in Puerto Rico for a year, so I knew Spanish really well. My Grandpa would get pissed when I would speak to my brothers in English. He would shake his hand at me and say, *"Habla me en Castellano."* I would ask him, "What is Castellano?" He then told me, *"Habla Espanol."* Then I knew what he was talking about.

A couple of more times, I would speak to my brother's in English, and he would shake his hand at me again, and after a while I would at first speak Spanish to my brothers even though I knew they didn't know what the hell I was saying, so I would speak to them in English and before Grandpa could react, I would translate what I had told my brothers. The strict rules of my Grandpa caused tension in the house, and I would hear my stepmom express her frustration about him. After about three years, my dad agreed to get them their own apartment.

So, as a result, whenever he asked me to help out with my grandparents, I never said no and never made excuses. Like him, I felt a sense of duty. Our parents take care of us, and our turn will come when it's time to take care of them. Besides, I remember I made the mistake of not helping out when they first moved into our house. I walked to the supermarket down the street. We started walking back. I was carrying the groceries.

My buddies drove by and said, "Let's go to the beach."

I asked my grandma if I could go. She said 'yes' and so I left. Later that day, my dad found out and he verbally let me have it. From that day, I learned to always help my grandparents.

I got in my truck and drove over to my grandparents apartment. After I parked my car I walked toward their apartment. As I approached, the paramedics were already there. I asked them where they would be taking him, and they told me Torrance Memorial. I looked at my grandma and she was worried. She explained what they were doing and how he fell. Then she asked me where they were taking him. Then I told her I was going to call my dad. I called my dad and told him what grandma told me, and that they were taking him to Torrance Memorial. When I told him where they were taking my grandpa, there was a pause and I knew he was even more worried. Then he finally said, "I'll meet you there," and I hung up the phone.

By the time I got off the phone, the ambulance drove off, so I didn't get a chance to get in ride with my grandpa. I just hoped my dad was not going to get pissed off about that and give me a bunch of grief. So, I asked my grandma if she wanted to go in my truck and go to the hospital. She told me that she wanted to wait for my dad and talk to him before she went to the hospital to see what was going on. I said ok, and walked to my truck and headed to the hospital.

This was around 11am. I spent most of the day with my grandpa. He was quiet for most of the time. Then he said that he was seeing a bunch of ants on the wall and that the ants were starting to crawl on his hands and arms. I knew that was the medication talking. He talked more, but none of it was making sense even though I understood what he was saying. I was struck by the look in his eyes the more he spoke. I started to feel sadness, but a low level of sadness, I guess because we were never close and connected like I would have wanted.

Plus, as far as what my dad did for him and my grandma, I just never felt like he was grateful for being taken care of. He acted like he was entitled, like my dad should take care of him for all the stuff he did for my dad and my uncle's. That may be the case, but it was just his attitude. It was done in a cold manner, and I never could connect with him. The nicest thing he ever said was two months prior to him falling when I came by to take him to his dialysis appointment. Out of respect and politeness, I asked him how he was doing. He said he was doing bad but that he would be better once all his grandkids went to college and be professionals. He said it in a very warm manner that he wanted the best for us. I just wished I could have seen that warmth toward my dad. Who knows, he may have shown a different side or that exact side when I wasn't around, but I sure didn't see that from him when it came to my dad.

The more I thought about that moment of warmth he showed to me and how hard my dad worked to take care of him and my grandma, the more empathy I felt for him. But I was still wondering why, knowing he was such a hard ass. Then, he was suddenly quiet. I noticed how he was looking at me but really wasn't. It was like he was looking through me. Like how military guys talk about the thousand

Chapter Nine

yard stare. It was as if he was looking through me to the wall behind me. There was this hollowness there. I realized at that moment that there was a possibility that this was it. My grandpa may die. It then kind of scared me.

About thirty minutes later, his vitals seemed to be acting up. At least that was my perception because the machines were going a bit haywire and nurses started to enter. They told me that he needed to be moved to the ICU unit. I was like 'Oh shit. What am I going to tell my dad?' So, I just followed the nurses wheeling him down to the ICU. They took them down there and I just waited for my dad.

About thirty minutes after that, not only did he show up but also my Uncle Pedro. They then met with the doctor while I stayed by my grandpa's side. At this point, my grandpa was unconscious. Then, after the doctor met with my dad and my uncle, they just looked absolutely stunned. My dad just put his hands on his hips and walked to my grandpa. Nothing was said for about 5-10 minutes.

My dad said in Spanish to my uncle, "All we can do is wait and have hope."

I looked at my dad. I never have seen him like this. So unsure of himself, so worried. My stepmom at times looked worried but I never saw my dad worried. I told him I'm gonna grab a coke from the vending machine. He barely nodded and I went to the vending machine.

I came back and the doctor was there again. Then suddenly the machine my grandpa was hooked up to started to go haywire. Again, a bunch of nurses and the doctors came in. They tried to revive him. They even brought out those electric paddles and yelled "clear," but nothing was working. We just sat there and stared. We were all frozen. As fast as they started, it seemed like it was quickly over. One nurse looked at the doctor and asked him to call it. It was 6:45pm.

The doctor turned to my dad and uncle and simply said, "We did everything we could, but I'm sorry."

My uncle and my dad just briefly looked at each other as if to say, "What the hell just happened?" My dad just furrowed his forehead. It seemed like he wanted to tell my uncle something, but his mouth just moved uncontrollably without any words coming out. They then looked at my grandpa and then I saw something that I'll never forget – my dad started to cry. It was the damndest shock to me. I had a mixed bag of emotions. Whenever I would cry as a kid, he would tell me to stop. Men don't cry. So, I was taken aback that he would say that to me and now he was crying, but at the same time I had this deep empathy. Losing anyone is tough, but to lose a parent. Wow, what can you say? He and my uncle stood there and cried. I was frozen. I didn't know what to do other than call my stepmom and tell her what happened. She asked me how my dad was doing. I told her Uncle Pedro was here and both of them were taking grandpa's death really hard. Even though grandpa's health was deteriorating, you can tell they were not expecting it. I really believed that they thought grandpa would pull through. I felt bad because the last moments I spent with him, I saw this coming, but I did not see the emotions my dad felt, did not see that coming at all.

A week later, we had the viewing before my grandpa's body was to be shipped back to Peru to be buried in the family plot. Many of my dad's friends and our uncles who made the trip for the viewing, shook hands and talked with my dad. When things settled down, my dad walked to the casket. For some reason, I watched my dad closely. He looked so lost and burdened by what he was feeling. He looked very heavy. I walked off to the side, where he could not see me but I could see his profile. He had this overwhelming look on his face that I'll never forget. It was the look of unfinished business. So many thoughts and emotions unresolved and left behind, never to be found again.

As I approached my off-ramp on the freeway, I snapped out of my reflection of the moments surrounding my grandpa's death. I'll never forget that look on my dad's face. I knew two things in that moment after reflecting on my dad when he looked on to my grandpa in his casket. First, I never wanted to someday look at my dad's casket in the same way. I know we were struggling, but I knew I did not want my dad dying with unfinished business between us and second if something happened to my dad I didn't want to wail in regret the way Cookie did when Uncle Rocco died. I wished that I would have said that to the therapist.

I got off the freeway and made a left on 182nd street, headed down toward Prairie Avenue. Just before I was able to make a left on Prairie, the light turned red. I thought about those two things and decided, 'Yeah, I'm going to make an appointment to go back to see Dr. Westfield.'

When I got home the first thing I did was call Dr. Westfield and left a message for her that I wanted to come back next week.

CHAPTER TEN

After that thought, I sat on my hospital bed and looked at the clock. It was 5:30. I thought I was about to get ready to leave because I saw the psychiatrist walking toward my room, and just before he walked in you can see by his body language and facial expression that he forgot something, so he walked out and back toward, I guess, his office.

"Shit," I said, "I want to get out of here. I want to be able to have dinner with my family."

So I had to wait longer, which didn't sit well with me because I knew other shit from my past was going to enter my mind I and would have to dwell even more on the situation. But truthfully, I felt fine, I told myself, I'm ready to go home. I don't think I need to spend any time in a mental care facility, especially if it's optional. I've already gone through years of therapy. I know what's going on, and I got over it. So I am ready to tell the psychiatrist that I am going to pass on his offer and just go home and get back to normal.

Then, I suddenly thought about the second nervous breakdown I had, which was about seven years earlier. It had happened regarding my niece from my half-brother. About three or four years before that, I reunited with my brother after he had years of resentment toward me when our mom, Cookie died. Our Aunt Doris was instrumental in reconnecting us. We met up at my aunt's house, and he was pissed to see me at first, but then we sat down and talked and things were good.

Then, he came up one weekend and spent it with me and my wife, who was my fiancé at the time. Everything was good the first day of the weekend, then things got weird. He slept for most of the remaining days. When he went back to my Aunt Doris' house, my wife revealed to me that she saw him doing drugs in the house and that is why he was sleeping so much. After that, we kind of just lost touch.

A couple of years later, my Aunt Doris told me he had a girlfriend and got her pregnant. After the baby was born, my brother and his girlfriend and his baby were living with my Aunt Doris. Doris had a falling out with her husband. Later, her husband revealed to me that he kicked her out because she got hooked on drugs again and that she and my brother were doing drugs in his house multiple times.

I then received a phone call from a person who worked for the Department of Child Services. She told me that my niece, my brother's daughter, landed in the hospital and almost died. She had sucked on a pipe that had residual crystal meth. She was now in the state's custody. After what happened to my niece, the representative kept in contact and told us that we, since we were the next of kin, have the opportunity and the possibility to adopt her.

One weekend we were told that my niece could spend a weekend with us. So we drove to San Diego to pick her up from her foster family at a Target parking lot. Honestly, I was worried since she never met us that she would not want to come with us, but the transition was smooth, and we took her back to our house in Long Beach.

The weekend was great. We took her to the park, she loved our cat, and she connected really well with our daughter. They played dress up together, and we took her to McDonald's play place. After that weekend, my wife and I talked at length about adopting her. After a week of discussion, I came back from running errands. I parked my car in the garage and suddenly I started to feel the same exact way I did when I had my first panic attack. It was so bad that I called 911 and had them pick me up a block away from our house. I called my wife on my cell phone and told her what happened.

Once I was cleared to leave the emergency room. I told her that the decision to adopt my niece triggered my panic attack. I told my wife that so many thoughts came through my mind if we adopted her. My biggest worry was once my brother would get out of jail he would come looking for her, and if he didn't get his way that he would try to hurt my family. I told my wife that I just couldn't put my daughter through that, to see some semblance of the violence I faced on a constant basis when I was a kid living with Cookie. I simply told my wife, I couldn't do it.

But in the end, it might not have mattered. About six months later, the representative told us that the court had given my niece's mother an opportunity to regain custody of her. The court said that if she can get through a three-month program and have proof of employment, she could get custody of her. The mother was able to meet the conditions of the court and she regained custody. Once she gained custody, she lasted three months. One of the conditions on top of her rehab and getting a job was not to have any contact with my brother.

For the first two months were easy because my brother was in jail, but once he got out, she ended up getting back into their drug routine, and she once again lost custody of my niece. They offered me another chance to adopt her, but right off the bat I knew I did not want to go through this again, so I told them it would be best if she were adopted by a good family, and eventually she was and we got a chance to see her a couple of years later. But I at least knew what triggered my second panic attack, but this most recent one still bothered me. I just didn't quite know what triggered this attack at
my work.

As I continued to sit in the hospital bed and finished the reflection of my second panic attack, the psychiatrist finally came into my room.

"Based on the information I have, I recommend a 72-hour hold," he said.

"I get it," I said, "but I'm feeling fine and I'm ready to go home."

"I really think you should check in for 72 hours."

"I'm gonna pass," I said. "I'm ready to get out of here."

"Ok, I have some paperwork for you to sign then you can head home."

"Thanks, Doc," I said.

CHAPTER ELEVEN

About a half an hour later, I was discharged. I sat on one of the benches in front of the emergency room and called my wife. She picked me up forty-five minutes later. She looked at me and asked me if I was all right. I told her that I felt fine and that I wanted to pick up my car and head out and get some dinner. I then asked her if our daughter knew what was going on. She told me that Mar didn't know anything. I told her good, that I didn't really want her to know.

About fifteen minutes later, my wife dropped me off at my car, and I drove home without incident. I honestly just enjoyed the ride over the two bridges and on to the 710 and transition to the 405 and got off on Orange avenue. I didn't really think much about what happened, I just thought about looking forward to going to dinner and spending time with my family. I did have a scary thought as I was waiting at the traffic light. I thought about how good my life had been up until the point of my panic attack, then I quickly thought about how everything I built just got leveled in an instant, but I'm going to make sure I rebuild it so I can be a better dad and husband, then the light turned green.

Once I got home, I changed my clothes and asked my family where they wanted to go. My daughter suggested the Hangar. The Hangar is located in this business park called Douglas Park. The old aerospace company called McDonnell Douglas used to own it and they eventually sold off the land. For years, there were rumors and discussions about what would be built. Finally, they built an outdoor mall surrounded by businesses including Virgin Orbit, a company that is building commercial space flight owned by the famous billionaire Richard Branson. In the middle of the outdoor mall is the Hangar at the Long Beach Exchange. It's a building that looks like an airplane hangar, but once you go in, there is an upscale food court inside. My wife took our daughter there one afternoon, and they had some gourmet grilled cheese sandwiches and my daughter has loved this place ever since, but tonight was my first night there and the set up was cool and it was really nice because the facility was just built a year and a half ago.

There were a ton of restaurants to choose from. They had a Nashville Hot Chicken spot, Korean BBQ, the Grilled Cheese place my family talked about, a sandwich place, and Mediterranean food. It was impressive the amount of places they had and the diversity of food. It was nice that they didn't have typical fast food places, like McDonald's or Jack in the Box.

We walked around to see what we wanted. My wife wanted the Korean BBQ. My daughter, of course wanted the gourmet grilled cheese, while I was torn between the Hot Nashville chicken and this place called The Kroft that had sandwiches and Poutine. They had a picture of Poutine with a fried egg on top. My wife and I always agree that anything with a fried egg on top is absolutely delicious. so I told my family that is where I wanted to eat.

We ordered our food and sat down to eat. As we ate, about halfway through our meal, I start to feel the same symptoms I felt when I was in front of my class. I got up and told my family that I was going to the bathroom. I started circling the building trying to calm down. I eventually calmed down but my nerves were still a wreck. I came back after a while and sat down but I was still struggling.

After dinner we drive home and parked the car in the garage. We went in the house and our dog, Gabe, rushed us. Her tail wagged insanely, we all took turns petting her.

"Are you ok?" my wife said.

"I thought I was," I said.

"Yeah, you looked a little freaked out at dinner."

"Yeah, once I was evaluated by the Psychiatrist, I felt fine."

"What did the psychiatrist say?"

"He evaluated me," I said. "He asked me questions about family history, was I on any medications, if there was a family of mental illness in the family…stuff like that." But I didn't want to tell her that the doctor recommended a 72-hour hold.

"Are you sure you are feeling fine?"

"I'm a little edgy," I said. "Probably residual nerves from my attack this afternoon."

"What do you think caused it?"

"Not sure," I said. "I mean, I can identify the exact cause of the two other attacks, but this one…it's the first time I am truly confused about it."

"I think a lot of it is your lack of sleep," she said. "I know you stayed up really late writing that letter to your parents."

"You think so?"

"Yeah," she said. "Maybe the info in the letter somehow triggered you."

"It kind of makes sense," I said. "I mean, I'll admit there was a lot of emotion put in the letter, and I did go to bed really late, but I guess why would that cause a panic attack? What I said in the letter was very positive. The other two panic attacks were triggered by negative situations."

"Yeah, I don't know but I feel that the lack of sleep had a lot to do with it," she said.

"Here comes Marli," I said. "Let's talk about it more later."

CHAPTER TWELVE

For the next two hours, it was pretty quiet. We were all watching TV and then my daughter got a text message and went to her room. I thought she didn't need to go to her room, it was a text message. It wasn't like it was a phone call. My wife and I just remained on the sofa and watched TV, when suddenly I started to feel really bad anxiety. I didn't feel like my blood pressure was rising and I wasn't feeling the anxiety level I felt when I called 911 to go to the hospital, but the anxiety was definitely stronger than it was during dinner.

"Can we go for a walk?"

"Yes," my wife said.

The more we walked the more my anxiety rose. It is hard to explain, but I was talking in patterns. I would ramble on and on and I honestly don't fully remember but at the end of each ramble I would say to my wife, "see it's a pattern." It was a strange feeling, I felt like physically I was losing control of my speech and thoughts. I would just blab out what I was thinking. I think I did say something about how people don't understand what homeless people go through, or what goes through their head but what I am going through in this moment may be what they are struggling with. Then I told her that all of this must seem weird to you, but this was the stuff that invaded my head when I would go through a panic attack. I also told her that I at least feel somewhat better because she was with me. I told her the two other panic attacks were really tough on me because I was alone both times, and it was very scary. It reminded me of when I was a kid. Most of the time I was left alone. It was fine during the day where I would just play throwing a baseball or a tennis ball and pretend I was in a major league game, but nights were the toughest because Cookie would leave me alone and she would not come home for hours. I was always terrified half the time. And after I would tell this to my wife I continued to repeat, "See it's a pattern."

This walking and talking went on for two hours before I felt sane and safe enough to go back home. My daughter was concerned, and I don't know what my wife said to her, but she used some excuse to tell her why we took so long. I was exhausted but not sleepy, so to calm my nerves and get some sleep I took some Nyquil. After about twenty minutes, I was able to fall asleep.

CHAPTER THIRTEEN

I abruptly woke up, causing my wife to wake up and I started pacing furiously back and forth. I felt like my soul was breaking through and crawling out of my body. I told my wife that we may need to call 911. A couple of more minutes pass. I feel like I am going insane. I then paced in the living room. I got dressed and asked her if we can go for a walk. After she changed and came into the living room, my panic attack increased even more. I told my wife to call 911 and I went and sat on the curb because I did not want my daughter to know that the paramedics were there for me. While I was sitting on the curb, my wife checked in on our daughter, who was thankfully already in her morning shower, and came back. I quietly entered the ambulance and watched my wife walk back inside.

At first, during the ambulance ride, I was quiet until the paramedic started to ask me questions. I tried to answer. I could feel my mouth and my muscles trying to answer his questions but nothing was coming out. I started to go into a manic state. I kept repeating, "May 9th, May 9th is when I had my nervous breakdown." I did this for a couple of minutes and I could see the look of confusion on the paramedics face. I was able to finally answer the question, and I explained to him that I can answer but my mind is stuck in a pattern. So even though I was able to answer the question, I had to start with "May 9th, May 9th is when I had my nervous breakdown." To the paramedic's credit, he was really patient with me. Patiently, he stuck by me and just kept asking me questions and he waited for my answer despite the manic state that I was in. Then they wheeled me on the gurney. I started literally fighting against my anxiety and manic state. I started having a boxing match thinking I'm going to win. I just kept punching in the air thinking that I was going to beat the shit out of my anxiety. I wouldn't have blamed anyone if they thought I was going crazy.

I again ended up in a hospital room for the second time in two days. I was conscious of everything around me. I was fully aware of everything but was mentally in a daze. I felt like I was on medication even though I wasn't. I was restless as hell, so I got out of the bed and paced back and forth like I was actually trying to get somewhere. Then a nurse came in and asked me questions. Honestly, I don't remember what I said, but then a doctor came in and continued to ask me a series of questions. I remembered nothing until she asked me if I wanted to hurt myself or hurt others. When she asked me that, normally I would say no. I might have even said, "Hell no." But for some reason I froze. I told her, "I don't know."

Sometime later, the psychiatrist that evaluated me the day before came in and looked concerned. "Here we are again," he said, but I did not take what he said in a judgmental way. I took it like he was genuinely trying to help me. He asked me what happened and I told him the whole story from having dinner with my family and feeling anxious, to the two-hour walk with my wife, to waking up and having a full-blown panic attack that landed me in my current situation.

"Well, I still think you should go into a 72-hour hold," he said.

"I don't want to admit it," I said, "but I think you're right. I'm really fucked up right now and I definitely can't go back to my wife and daughter like this."

"I'll get everything set up," he said. "Just sit tight."

I waited and waited wondering what was going to happen next. I noticed now that they posted a security guard outside my room. I was fine for a while then I got up and started pacing furiously back and forth around my bed. I thought again about the female doctor asking me if I wanted to hurt myself and hurt others, then I thought about all the shit that just happened to me over the course of a day and a half, and suddenly got pissed off. Again, my nerves started to take over, but I felt angry with the nerves. I suddenly stopped pacing and looked over at the security guard. For some reason, I had this urge like I wanted to rush him, I wanted to take a shot at him. I just don't know why, I can't explain it but I felt that way. It felt like the climax of the movie "Lethal Weapon," with Mel Gibson when he confronts the villain played by Gary Busey. He then asks Gary Busey's character if he wants a shot at the title, and Gary Busey said, "I don't mind if I do," and he starts to roll up his sleeves and rushes Mel Gibson. At that moment, I felt like that Gary Busey character, like I wanted a shot at the title.

I walked toward the door. Not quickly, but not slowly. Then the security guard and I locked eyes. As soon as that happened, he got up off his chair. When I got closer to the door, I suddenly stopped. Thank God my senses started to take over and I started to be rational. I realized, "Why do I want to rush this guy? He hasn't done anything to me. He is just doing his job. Why would I want to take that away from him? Why do I want to make his day more difficult than it has to be?" I looked him in the eye and simply said, "Can you just talk to me?"

He stood about three feet from the doorway. He knew that he needed to be wary of his safety but at the same time respect my space. He then looked at me and said, "Yeah, I can do that."

"I feel really fucked up," I said. "Do you see me as a threat?"

"No. We're fine because we haven't even wrestled yet," he said with a smile. "If we were wrestling then we would have a problem."

"How long have you worked security?"

"For about three years," he said.

"Is this long term for you?"

"No," he said. "I also go to school."

"What school?"

"El Camino College."

"Oh yeah, I went to ELCO, but way back in the day."

"When was that?"

"Back in '89-'90," I said. "I played football for two years."

"Did you play football after that?"

"Nah, I got burned out. It became like a job, and I fell out of love with it. I got lost when I realized that football wasn't going to be my future. So what are you studying?"

"Criminal justice," he said. "I want to become a cop."

"Oh yeah? My brother is a cop."

"Where at?"

"Gardena PD," I said. "He's been a cop for almost eighteen years. He served in the Marine Corps before that."

"Cool," he said. After that, I could feel my nerves and emotions settling down. I then felt tired but not sleepy. I turned and said, "Thanks for talking to me."

He said, "No problem," and I got back in the bed and just stared at the ceiling.

I started to pray frantically. I flashbacked as far as my faith journey, when I converted to becoming a Catholic. In my interview, my principal, who also happened to be a priest, asked me if I had any anti-Christian sentiments or anything against the Pope of the Catholic Church. I told him no. Then, I think it was in my second year, I was called into his office. It surrounded a situation where abortion had come up.

My students asked me what I thought about the whole issue. I told them, "I don't know because I am not a woman. I wouldn't know what I would do in that situation because biologically I can't have kids." That did not sit well with him. At first, I didn't understand why because I remained neutral, that I hadn't taken a side. He then said I could not answer that way because it was moral relativism. I looked at him and asked "Moral what?"

"It's basically being neutral toward moral standards. That there is no room for judgment. That there really is no distinction of right or wrong. The church teaches us that there is no gray area when it comes to abortion. It is absolutely against the teaching of Jesus and the church. That is what has to be expressed to the students. We are pro-life, not pro-voice."

"Oh, ok. I'm sorry I didn't mean to offend. I mean personally, if I got someone pregnant I wouldn't want for them to have an abortion, but since I am not carrying the child I feel I have no say."

"I understand, and that is entirely another discussion for another time, but my suggestion is just avoid this topic and other controversial topics."

"Fair enough," I said. Then I felt bad because the year before, we talked about the Sixth Commandment, Thou shall not kill, and I questioned and had made the remark, "Well God, in the Old Testament, kills everyone."

From that point forward, I started to pay more attention to morality and spirituality. I started to closely examine faith itself. I started off studying Zen and Buddhism and tried that, but it didn't feel right.

We attended the Self-Realization Fellowship Center, which was founded by Yogi Paramahansa Yogananda. The location near us was the Lake Shrine in the Palisades. It was such a beautiful and peaceful place, and we enjoyed the services, but the drive was too much for us. Then we tried my wife's faith. She was Methodist, and the walk was only about three minutes away from our house, but the daycare situation was difficult. We needed daycare because we knew our daughter could not sit still. We tried for about three months, but it didn't last. So I went back to square one.

I decided to start attending, on my own, the morning masses that were offered before school started. Even though I had no plan on being Catholic at the time, I enjoyed the energy I had afterwards in facing my day. I felt good. But I also felt left out during communion time. Because I was not confirmed I could not take communion. I would go up and cross my arms for a blessing, but I still felt left out watching everyone else taking communion.

My morning mass went on for about six months. Then I came home. There were days when I would come home and I had something serious to talk to my wife about.

She would joke with me, "What, are you becoming Catholic?"

So one particular day, I came up to her after getting home from work and putting my work stuff away and changing out of my work clothes, I told her, "I have a confession."

"What, you wanna become Catholic?"

I paused. "Yes."

"Really?"

Yes."

"Ok," she said. "When did you decide this?"

"Well, I have been going to morning masses at the school for the past six months. I guess I just feel a connection. It has brought me back to a spirituality. I feel like I'm coming home by making this decision if that makes sense."

"Yeah, it does," she said.

"Look, this is something I want to do," I said. "I don't expect you to convert with me. That is the last thing I want to do is impose my spirituality on you." She took a long pause on what I said.

Finally, she said, "Look, we are a couple. We are a team. We made a commitment to each other. I think we should explore this together."

"Really?"

"Yes."

Excited, I approached my principal the next day and told him my wife and I wanted to convert.

He smiled. "For you it's not a conversion because you were baptized Catholic. You are what we call a revert." He then asked what brought about my wanting to take this step.

"Working here made me want to explore my spirituality. So I went on a journey exploring different faiths but as good as all the other faiths were, I felt a strong connection when I started to attend mass in the mornings. I felt like I was home." All he could do was smile.

"Ok, let's get you started on your path."

Six months later, my wife and I became full members of the church. A couple of months later, we got our daughter baptized and had our marriage blessed by the church. I then thought about a vision I had several months after we were part of the church. There was a Marian mass in honor of the Virgin Mary. Right before communion, as the priest said the Eucharistic prayer, I closed my eyes like I normally do. Then, suddenly I saw Cookie huddled in the corner. It looked like she was in one of the rooms in my grandma Carmen's house in Puerto Rico. She was curled up and shaking with her head buried in her knees. Then she looked up at me and said, "Sorry," then I saw the Virgin Mary take her to heaven.

As I sat there on the edge of the hospital bed waiting to be taken to the mental health facility, I started to pray. One time I was starting to have a panic attack and I kept praying the Hail Mary and the anxiety went away. So I prayed hoping for the same result. But it seemed like the anxiety got worse. I prayed harder and harder for the Hail Mary but it wasn't working.

After a while, my mind went blank and I just sat there with my mind going quiet. I felt like Cookie, like I was in a dark corner of nothingness, like I was in solitary confinement or worse maybe Purgatory. I suddenly imagined I was in front of God and asked Him, "What's the point?" but I asked it in a way where I wasn't expecting an answer. I then just laid down from exhaustion.

CHAPTER FOURTEEN

I was lying in bed and just staring blankly at the ceiling. The nurses attempted to give me medication and I'd lose my shit and scream. I did not want to take it, but they insisted I needed it and noticed my agitation, so they both left the room. One nurse came back later and told me my wife was here. I told him I wanted my wife to give me my medication.

My wife came into the room and comforted me. The nurse gave my wife the medication. She attempted to give it to me but I got into a manic pattern. She immediately recognized what was going on.

My penchant for relying on patterns started up again. I started looking at the clock. I counted the little hand then looked at my wife. I think I had to take two or more pills. It seemed lke slow motion for me to move toward my wife.

I felt like I took forever, but I did take all of my medication. I told her that I tried to pray my anxiety away and after feeling too exhausted to pray that I thought I lost my faith in God, at least for a moment. But I didn't want lose faith. Especially when I looked at her because I know there is a God because I see God when I see her face. After I said that, I felt a sudden calmness because for the first time in a day and a half I felt peace and I was able to finally go to sleep without feeling like I was going to die.

I don't know how long I was asleep, but my wife woke me up to tell me that the psychiatrist was there and told me that the ambulance was ready to take me. I hugged my wife and we cried together and she said, "I'll see you in a few days, and I will call you as soon as I can." I didn't want to leave. I felt so heartbroken. I felt so defeated. I always thought I was tough and that because of what I went through with Cookie, that I could stand up to anything that stood in my way. This was the first time I felt like life kicked my ass, that life found a way to conquer my fighting spirit. I remember seeing documentaries or films about soldiers being in prisoner of war camps and the talk about how their captors broke them. I told myself as I was watching those films, 'that would never happen to me.' But yet, here I am and it did happen to me and I never felt as lost and broken as I did after saying goodbye to my wife.

The ambulance drove to the hospital. I felt empty and wanted to cry but just felt too empty to cry. I looked out of the ambulance window. I saw a woman who looked like my wife at a bus stop. I wanted to call out and reach out to her even though I knew it was not my wife.

There was another time I felt like I wanted to reach out for help. It was when I was ten years old and was living with Cookie at my uncle's house in San Sebastian, Puerto Rico, a town that is toward the west coast of the Island, about ten miles from the coastal town of Aguadilla.

At the time, Cookie worked nights as a bartender. While she was at work, I would hang out in the streets at late hours of the night. I kept doing it because my grandma's brother was too old to look after me as he went to bed early, and he probably didn't care what I was doing out of the house. Somehow, though, Cookie got wind of the fact that I was out on the streets after she went in to work. She told me that she knew and that I better not do it again, but I didn't listen.

About a week later, I got home, and I nearly shit my pants when I saw Cookie standing in the doorway of the kitchen.

She calmly walked over to me. "What did I tell you about being in the streets at night?"

"You told me to be inside when you went to work," I said.

"Why aren't you in the house?"

"I...I don't know."

Out of nowhere and with cat quick reflexes she punched me in my right eye then grabbed me by the back of my shirt and dragged me to my room. In that house and on a couple of doors, you see something

Chapter Fourteen

that you don't see in most houses and that is a lock on the outside of a bedroom door. Unfortunately, this was a bedroom with an outside lock. She pushed me in the room and locked the door behind me.

The next morning she opened the door but didn't let me out. She came in with a tray that had a plate full of bread that was spread with butter and a pitcher of water and an empty glass. She barely looked at me only to tell me "here" and placed the tray on my table near the window and walked out without saying a word. I thought she would feel bad and maybe an hour later finally let me out of the room, but that didn't happen. I knew I was already in there for a couple hours at least even though there were no clocks in the room. I could tell by the shadows by the creek that flowed near our house. Plus, people were allowed to throw trash out of their windows to the creek below, and I saw that there was more trash than when Cookie came in to give me my bread and water.

After a while, I did get hungry, and so I ate all of my bread and drank all of the water. When I was done, I looked out of the window and out to the creek. I then saw three figures walking along the side of the creek. I saw three of my classmates. One was a girl named Wanda. I thought she was the prettiest girl in the school. She had blue eyes and very curly hair like the child star Shirley Temple, and she wore her usual overalls, which were green. I think she had overalls of every color for each day of the week. With her was her older brother Felix and their cousin, the neighborhood bully, a kid we all called Firecracker. No one, outside of Wanda and her brother, knew his name but they never told us because they were worried about getting their ass kicked. They walked about half a mile, sat by the side of the creek, and pulled out some cigarettes. I opened the window wanting to call out to them to help me somehow. But I froze. I was worried about Cookie hearing me. God, I desperately wanted to call out for them to get me out of here, but I also knew that Firecracker was not a big fan of mine because Wanda used to be my girlfriend and he was very protective of her.

I closed the window and went back and lay on my bed quietly and stayed that way for another day thinking that I needed some type of miracle. Then on the third day Cookie opened the door and left it open. I got up and went to make something for myself for lunch.

CHAPTER FIFTEEN

The next morning, I heard a voice say that breakfast was ready. I was still half asleep so couldn't see who it was. It sounded like a female, and I'm sure by the tone that it was a staff member. I picked my head up and physically felt like I could not get up. I simply just went back to sleep. The same voice came in later and announced that lunch was ready. I barely moved again and just went back to sleep. What seemed like a couple of hours passed and the same person asked me if I wanted to go to group, but I just put my head down and went back to sleep. It wasn't that I was being anti-social or I didn't want to eat, or confront my issues. I was good at confronting my issues having learned that from years of therapy. Emotionally and psychologically, I wanted to go to group, but what I just experienced had completely drained me.

It was more than my body giving out on me, I felt like my soul was exhausted and spent, like I had nothing left to give right now. I felt bad I didn't go to group and I felt bad about not eating but I just did not have any energy and I wondered if I was even going to get up at some point today but I had my doubts, until about evening time, just before dinner and I believe dinner was at six, my roommate walked in.

"Are you William?"

"I go by Hector," I said, "but my paperwork says William."

"You got a phone call," he said.

"Thanks," I said and suddenly got this small, renewed ounce of energy, enough to get me to sit up in my bed and look at my daughter's wallet-sized volleyball photo. I picked up the photo and headed over to the common room where the phone was located. I took a look at the common area just before sitting down. There were about ten to fifteen people hanging out. They're all doing different things. Some are watching a basketball game on the T.V., others were playing cards, others are coloring and drawing and some are sitting by the window staring at the L.A. cityscape in the distance. I sat down and picked up the phone.

"Hello?"

"Hi, honey," my wife said.

"I love you," I said.

"I love you too," she said. "How ya doin?"

"Not sure, I just woke up," I said. "I've been sleeping the whole day. I feel a little guilty."

"Why?"

"I guess because I was raised by my dad to be productive," I said. "His old saying growing up was, 'The lazy person always works twice.'"

"Don't worry about that," she said. "You need the rest. You've been through a lot."

"It's been a bit rough," I said. "I had a hard time settling down and getting to sleep. Remember the way I paced back and forth manically when I was in the living room when I asked you to call 911?"

"Yeah," she said.

"It felt worse last night. I paced from my room down the hallways to the lunch area. I honestly thought if I kept pacing that I would calm down enough, I would be able to come home."

"I'm sorry," she said.

"Then, I really thought they were going to stick me in a straightjacket. I wouldn't go to bed when the staff asked me too. I started to get really agitated, and for a split second I wanted to fight them. I just wanted to come home because I felt that once I went to sleep here, I knew for sure I wouldn't come home for a couple of days. I missed you and Mar. Missing you guys is killing me, and I am doing everything in my power to get back to you guys."

"You're gonna come back home and when you do you are going to be better," she said.

"But what if I'm not?"

"Everything will work out. You will deal with your demons while you're getting care and you're going to come back home a better man."

"But I feel like I'm not," I said. "Based on what's happened, I feel less like a man."

"But you're not," she said. "It's just the rawness of everything you have been through the last couple of days that's causing you to feel that way."

"I keep asking staff members if I am going insane."

"And what do they say?"

"They say no, that they have seen a lot worse."

"See, you're going to be ok. I promise. When she said that I felt a sense of calm. A temporary moment of normalcy.

"How's our daughter doing?"

"I vaguely told her what happened. Of course she's worried, but she feels good that you are being taken care of."

"That's good. Look, I already feel bad that I am not going to be home for Mother's Day but please don't cancel the Mother's Day brunch. I know it's going to be tough on you and Mar, but I would have peace of mind knowing you and Mar are around family. You guys need that support and I just want you and our daughter, for a moment, to not dwell on my situation. I know it's easier said than done. That's one thing I want from you and Mar is to go to the Mother's Day brunch. Can you and her do that for me?"

"Absolutely," she said.

"I think she has a volleyball tournament tomorrow, doesn't she?"

"Yeah," she said.

"Make sure you take some video for me," I said.

"Oh, I will," she said. I love you with all my heart and soul. You are the man of my dreams."

"Thank you," I said. "That's a lot to process right now."

"I know," she said.

"Especially when I feel that I'm going crazy."

"You're not going crazy. Trust me."

"I do, I'm just having trouble trusting the world and the circumstances around me."

"But the only way you get through this is you have to trust the people that are helping you, or it's going to be harder on you. Look at it this way – the more you trust yourself and the people helping you, the quicker you'll come home."

"True," I said. "I want to be on the phone with you all night but dinner is coming up and I haven't eaten anything for the past day and a half and I'm starving now."

"I know, honey. Get something to eat and get rest, Get as much rest as you can. Remember you are not lazy."

"Ok," I chuckled.

"I love you," she said. "Do you want me to call you tomorrow after the tournament?"

"That would be great to hear your voice again."

"Ok, love," she said. "I will be praying for you, and I will call you tomorrow. Bye Honey."

"Bye sweety," I said and hung up the phone.

CHAPTER SIXTEEN

As soon as I hung up the phone, the nurses announced that dinner was ready. So, I got up and headed to the dining hall. They were serving fish with green beans and fruit punch and chocolate pudding. I took the cover off of my plate. The fish was ok but lacked seasoning. I asked for salt. The nurse paused and looked at the information that was on the side of my plate.

"You can't have salt," she said.

"Why?"

"Because you are on cholesterol medicine," she said.

"What's the big deal?"

"Doctor's orders. You can't have salt." She walked away abruptly.

As I was eating, I looked at the people around me. I noticed that my roommate was sitting right across from me. He ate quietly. Other people around the table discussed the food. Some complained, but others liked what they were eating. They were also talking about playing cards after dinner. I was starting to feel a little bit normal being around people and listening to them talk. I still wanted to go home but was more rational about my situation. After I was done eating, I actually went to the common room. Honestly, I didn't know what I was going to do in the common room, but I knew that I didn't want to go back to my room right away. I kind of saw that as a good sign. Once I finished, I cleared my tray and put the tray back into the tray holder and walked over to the common room.

I sat for the first time in the common room. It was strange. I mean I walked by it many times, especially that first night I was here. It was like being at a zoo, you could see the interactions of the animals up close and personal but there was always a barrier of some type, either a ravine or glass. I just would look from afar, see faces, people walking, watching TV, they seemed more like images, but now it was different, it was like I was in real time, it was *real*, and what I mean by that is that I could see the color of people's hair, the facial expressions, the lines in some people's faces, that some people missing teeth, the pensiveness of some people's foreheads, some people scratching their noses and eyebrows.

I just sat and observed the people but was observing their actions. It seemed that they were in clusters. One cluster was playing cards, another cluster was drawing and sketching, another cluster coloring, another cluster watching TV. There were a couple of stragglers but not too many but out of the stragglers I did notice one sitting by himself looking out the window. He was an African-American male maybe in his mid-forties. The way he was sitting by the window and how he rested his left hand on his elbow. It looked very similar to me. It reminded me of Cookie as far as I didn't know, but I assumed he was a smoker. Then there was a white lady, with long gray hair, maybe in late fifties, wearing a black sweater over a medical smock. She kept kind of pacing around the table talking out loud. Actually, it was more like mumbling because I could not understand a word she was saying, but she looked very agitated.

Then I was distracted by another white woman that was sitting in front of me. She was the one that had missing teeth, she mumbled something to me.

"What?" I said.

"iZZ thet yr daughter?"

I was holding my daughter's volleyball picture in my hand. I just nodded.

"Kin I see?"

I then showed it to her, and I don't know if it was intentional or not but I thought she was trying to reach out for the picture, and I snatched my hand back as quick as I could and momentarily felt pissed. As I look back, I don't remember if she was trying to reach out for it or not but there was a hand movement, and by the look on her face she noticed the suddenness of moving my hand away that she just

Chapter Sixteen

let things be and started to observe the woman who was pacing and mumbling to herself.

Once I noticed I looked at the art supplies on the table. I looked at the crayons, colored pencils, blank sheets of paper and the coloring books. I wasn't going to grab the blank papers and the pencils because I was horrendous at art, so I looked over several of the coloring books. They had the Transformers, Superfriends, Disney ones, and Ninja Turtles. I reached over for the Ninja Turtles. I missed my dog a little bit, and the Turtles were the closest thing to a pet I could think of even though they were wielding swords and battle gear and following a rat as their mentor. I opened it to see what pages were not colored on and found a scene where they were running down the street after one of their enemies. Then I noticed the woman missing her teeth kept staring at the one pacing around the table. After the pacing woman made about three turns around the table, she then started to stare down the toothless woman sitting in front of me. I had a bad feeling like this was not going to go well.

The pacing woman now just stayed in the corner that had the TV hanging from above. She still continued to pace back and forth but it was in that area and she paced back and forth from one wall to another instead of around the table and she kept staring at the toothless woman but the pacing woman's mumbling got slightly louder, then the mumbling became to like a slurred speech and grunting but you can hear at the end of her attempted formulation of a sentence was "Fuckin . ..ahh . . .shit."

"Fockkk you," the toothless woman said.

The pacing woman then flipped off the toothless woman and continued to pace then looked at her again. "Bitch," the pacing woman said. But this time she was louder when she said.

Then the toothless woman stood up, "You fockin bicchh." Even though she stood up she didn't make any movement toward the pacing woman. It was as if she was just waiting to say the right word or make the right gesture to trigger the toothless woman to charge the pacing woman.

At that point, the nurses came in from their stations to see what was going on. I was expecting the nurses to say something, but one stood by the pacing woman and one stood just over the shoulder of the toothless woman, but I noticed that they still gave the ladies space for them to not get even more agitated.

The ladies seemed at first to calm down. At least the toothless woman started to slowly sit down but for some reason just the mere presence of the nurses seemed to agitate the pacing woman, and she slurred out, "Whore!"

In my mind, I was like, 'Oh shit,' and before she even sat all the way down she started to charge but to the nurses' credits, they grabbed each of them. It was like a pair of rams on a mountain ready to lock horns, and suddenly they were both roped and pulled by the horns before they could collide. Then each of them escorted the two women out of the room. I didn't know quite what to think of it other than to just color, and that is what I did for the next couple of hours. I mean I didn't just color for two hours. I also watched TV. I think they had it on the Celtics and Spurs game. But I only watched in stretches because as a Lakers fan I couldn't stand the Celtics. I only watched when the Spurs were ahead, but when the Celtics tied or regained the lead, I stopped watching.

I felt tired, and it was almost lights out anyway. I decided to walk back to my room. My roommate stayed behind and continued to watch TV. Once I went back to my room I gently placed my daughter's photo on the nightstand. I took a look at the L.A. skyline. I know it doesn't compare to New York's, but it could still hold its own. At least there were gaps on either side of the skyline and not compact and on top of each other like New York. I felt with the L.A. skyline, there was more of a sense of freedom. It was L.A. but it was other things when you saw the gaps on each side of the skyline. It was other cities and other communities. When you looked at the New York skyline it was only New York. Regardless, I loved both skylines.

Then I looked down from the skyline to the parking lot below and at the entrance to the parking lot and I noticed a fire hydrant.

The hydrant reminded me of when I was about eight years old. The day after Cookie got into it with her boyfriend Papo, they talked shit out and decided to take me to the boardwalk in Atlantic City. The day started off okay, nothing out of the ordinary, but then it was like an omen once we got there. To cut through traffic, Cookie had a bad habit of recklessly going down one way streets. The scary thing was she drove like she was entitled to go down a one way. She drove with a fearlessness like nothing was ever going to happen. We approached a major boulevard and it was one way. I could see it in her eyes that she was going to do it. But this time it scared the shit out of me already because in the past, most of the time they were one, sometimes two lane one way streets. This time it was a four lane boulevard. She floored the fuckin thing into oncoming traffic. I really thought we were going to die. It seemed like we dodged at least ten cars. The fucked up thing, despite what she did I truly thought it was a miracle we made it through without any cars crashing into each other or the dividers and the craziest part, we never got pulled over by the cops. But I had a feeling that this was the first step toward some fucked up shit we may face.

We then went to the boardwalk. We walked the pier, then we checked out all the games and rides. I tried that ring toss. The air rifles. I wanted to win something. Everything was going great in my mind. Papo was talking to me about the Yankees. Cookie seemed to be smiling. Then I wanted to go to the baseball toss. I felt it was my best chance to win a prize. Honestly, I didn't care about the prize, I just wanted to win. It was the competitive nature that was in my DNA. The prize, honestly, I don't remember, but it was either Batman- or Superman-related because they were my all-time favorite superheroes. I was so happy until I turned around to talk to Papo, and he had a cold stare on his face. And then I wondered where the hell Cookie was. I looked over to the hot dog stand, and there she was holding the hot dogs but talking to some guy. I had no idea what they could be talking about, but I knew it wasn't good because even though Papo had brown skin, I could see his face turn red and I knew some bad shit was going down.

We continued to walk around the boardwalk but it was dead quite other than Cookie asking me if I was having a good time. These were the rare moments that Cookie ever gave a shit about me. She tried to talk to Papo but Papo at this point was completely shut down. Cookie kept asking him "What the fuck is wrong?" He kept mumbling "nothin," and when it got dark we headed to the car, and I did not think anything of it until Papo started the car and said, "Why the fuck were you talkin to that muthafucka." A normal person might try to answer or ask a question "Why are you talkin to me like that?" or shelve it for later when I wasn't around them. But Cookie was not normal.

"It's not yo muthafuckin business who the fuck I talk to," she said. "Last time I checked we ain't married."

"But you need to have respect," he said. "You're my woman."

"Listen, I ain't anybody's woman," she said. "I'm my own woman, and you are my man until I say you're not my man."

"What the fuck does that mean?"

"It means that if you don't like it you can get the fuck on," she said.

"Bitch, are you saying you don't need me?"

"I don't need any muthafucka and don't you forget it *cabron*!"

"Fuck you!"

Cookie paused. For some reason whatever boyfriend she had, she always knew how to push their buttons. She yelled back.

"You ain't shit. Fuck you and the mother that raised you."

Papo suddenly stopped the car and stared at Cookie. He stared at her like he was daring her to say something. There was a long pause.

"My mother?"

"You heard me," she said.

Then he reared his hand back and gave her one of the loudest slaps I have ever heard. I think that people on the boardwalk heard it. I don't normally get stunned because this is not the first time Cookie was hit, but I never heard it that loud. I thought '*Damn, that probably would shut her up*,' but she took her fist and punched him in the mouth as hard as she could. Suddenly it looked like Ali versus Frazier.

While that was going on, the car coasted slowly toward the corner, and suddenly we hit a fire hydrant. Water shot up all over the place, but Cookie and Papo kept battling for another five minutes until they heard faint sirens and Papo focused his energy getting us out of there. We made a couple of turns and thought we were clear, then the cops surrounded us and pulled out their guns. I was terrified and remembered from all the movies and TV shows I watched to put my hands in the air as fast as I could so they would not shoot us. But then the strangest thing I ever experienced happened to me.

In all the chaos, Cookie managed to calmly turn to me and say, "Put your fuckin' hand down. They ain't gonna do shit to us."

She was right. They didn't.

They took all of us to the station. An officer sat next to me and asked me about my Batman toy I had won at the boardwalk. I told the officer how much I loved Batman and Robin and how they battled the Joker and Penguin.

About an hour later, Cookie walked out, then Papo. I was really confused.

One of the cops asked Cookie, "You sure you don't wanna press charges?"

She, with her back turned to the officer and without missing a beat, raised her left arm and flipped him off.

I wondered why she stayed with this guy. It was later revealed by one of my cousins that Cookie told him that she couldn't be with a guy that she could dominate or beat the shit out of. If the guy couldn't fuck her up and put her in her place, she couldn't be with them. That's probably why Papo left the next day without telling us; never

Chapter Sixteen

to return. I was exhausted and felt like Papo; I quietly wanted to l eave but knew I had to stay because I loved my family and wanted to get back to them. I want to leave on my terms not out of fear of being uncomfortable.

After staring at the fire hydrant, I lie in bed. I just thought of being at home. Hugging my wife, hugging my daughter, petting my dog and giving her a treat. Maybe sitting in the back yard with my wife around the fire pit having smores and enjoying drinking some Maker 46 bourbon. I must miss doing the simple things. About a month before, I planned Mother's Day brunch for all the moms in our immediate family at the Lakewood Country Club. I hated that I was going to miss our get together with all the moms.

About five minutes later, an Asian staff woman came in and told me that one of the psychiatrists wanted to meet with me. I got up and left my room and made a right turn. Just before getting to the end of the hallway, I saw a man with a white doctor's coat and a clipboard waiting by a doorway that was to my right and his left. As I got closer, I was expecting him to say hello or ask me how I was doing and he just gestured for me to enter the office.

The fucking office was crammed. There was a table that looked like it used to be used at an elementary school. There was a blue plastic chair on one side and a nice office chair on the other. The psychiatrist sat down, then I sat down on the plastic chair.

When we sat, he didn't even make any eye contact. He just started looking at his clipboard. I imagine he was looking over notes summarizing what happened to me. After he finished looking over his notes, he then looked up at me and still did not greet me warmly or ask me how I was doing. He seemed really cold, and it started to agitate me especially when he just launched into a bunch of questions.

It was obviously an evaluation, but I was still kind of reeling and disoriented from my experience even though I felt a lot better than when I arrived here. I also remember that he had a thick accent. It sounded very Eastern European like he was either German or Russian. I'm not an expert in accents; it just sounded that way from all the movies and television shows I have watched over the years.

The more questions he asked I could feel myself more agitated.

For those 1980s television fans, he looked like Mr. Shrofosky from the television show *Fame*. Same glasses, same build, same styled gray hair. I try not to be judgmental, but he seemed like an asshole right off the bat, which surprised me because I did not think I could be judgmental in the vulnerable state that I was in.

I was aware of what was going on. He was asking a bunch of questions to assess my state of mind. To tell you the truth, I did not remember a lot of the questions he asked or how I answered. But what I do remember is that I said that I believed in God.

For some strange reason, he decided to say, "God does not exist."

I had to pause for a moment. It was a shocking pause. Like the movie *The Brothers McMullin* that was directed by and starred in by Edward Burns. The main character played by Ed Burns has two brothers, one older and one younger. The older brother has a conversation with the younger about infidelity, and it became a moral and philosophical discussion on why it's not good to have an affair, and suddenly the older brother says to the younger one, who is a devout Catholic, "Fuck God!" The older brother keeps rambling on, and the younger brother is bewildered and repeats with a question, "Fuck God?" It was like a kick in the balls to the younger brother. He was so shocked that someone could even think that.

I had that type of pause and shock even though the doctor continued with the questions. I then came back to my senses and slammed my fist on the table and yelled, "God does exist."

He then abruptly got up and said, "We are done."

As he got up, he gestured to a couple of male security people, and they said that I could now go back to my room.

I got up but slammed my chair against the door and walked out and one of the staff members put his hand on my shoulder to guard me against the doctor. I wanted to yell at him to get his hands off me, but my body was so exhausted that I was in no shape to get into an altercation so I just quickly left the doctor's office and headed back to my room.

CHAPTER SEVENTEEN

The doctor told me that God didn't exist. It really messed with my head, as I lay in bed staring out of the window thinking about my journey with God. I've had an interesting relationship with God. I was ingrained from the very beginning that God did exist and someday we are going to meet God in heaven, but Cookie and my Grandma Carmen always made it a point – and I don't know if it was conscious or unconscious –that we are going to suffer in getting there. We are going to take our beatings in order to reach the promised land.

There was a lot of irony to all of it when I think about it. Cookie and Grandma Carmen were great at preaching the word but definitely did not practice what they preached. They always talked about how God was good and how Christ is our savior. But every day they were in yelling matches and even having fist fights. I remember one time when they were fighting about something. I think Carmen was talking shit to Cookie about how she was raising me and Cookie lost her shit and snapped. At the time Carmen had a broken leg. She grabbed Carmen's broken leg and pushed her out of the front door of the apartment. She then grabbed her bible, went in the kitchen and was saying some prayer and put water in a bowl and went around saying blessings around the house and was throwing holy water everywhere including on me. And then she looked at me and said, "See, that is the devil at work."

But my first lesson was when I was about five. Cookie and I were living with Grandma Carmen at the time, and by living with her Cookie had a license to leave me with Grandma every night and wouldn't come home until late or some nights not at all. I started to have nightmares. I dreamed that the devil was under my bed every night waiting for me to get out of bed so he could grab me from under the bed and pull me down to hell. I told my Grandma, and she grabbed her Bible and prayed over me until I fell asleep. I knew at that moment that God did exist, but it was always complicated.

After those earlier experiences, I started to learn that basically, no matter what, this world is an evil place and the only time you will be happy is when you die and hope to get into heaven. All Cookie talked about was she couldn't wait to get to paradise, but in the same breath she was an addict and would not honor her responsibilities, especially taking responsibility in raising me. Sometimes she'd sit by the window getting drunk and tell me how the world is evil and only God was going to get us out of this, but she couldn't figure out how to get her and I out of this situation. She even tried to commit suicide.

Over time, I just did not know what to think. My dad at least tried. Once I moved in with him, he tried to take me to church, but he only took me on Christmas and Easter and during lent we would not eat meat on Fridays, but he would do the sign of the cross every time we got in the car, but other than that there was not much talk about faith. So, after that point living with my dad I didn't really talk or engage about faith other than I did believe in God but only said a prayer when I was desperate.

Then that seemed to change for me once I got into college and started to go to therapy. In therapy, I had to examine everything I had ever learned about life. My home life, my social life, my life in America, my life in my Latino Culture, my academic life, I had to examine all of it and many instances had to break down walls and rethink and possibly change many mindsets that were established within me over time, including how I looked at God, or higher power, or however people wanted to define the life force that was bigger than who we are.

In my first couple of years in therapy, the more I learned to empower myself and be vocal with the mindsets and perceived constraints of my true self, the more I started to question my family culture and structure. I found it empowering and beautiful. I held on tightly, but I definitely questioned how we tended to judge others.

In an ironic twist, I did the same thing. The more I empowered myself, the more I questioned my faith, particularly the faith life established by Cookie and my Grandma Carmen. I started to feel that religion was a crutch that did not allow you to embrace or look at self-awareness of self-discovery. But at the same time what I did not realize is religion can be very good. It can spark self-awareness and discovery. I had, particularly at that time, judgments against faiths.

Plus, I read about the religious philosophies and of how the Romantic poets viewed God – that He can be found in every aspect in nature, and that is the way to commune with God. I later learned that some of them smoked opium to arrive at that realization and I was not willing to alter my mind in that way.

So, I felt like I was abandoning religion. I was not interested in pursuing religion or reading the Bible to have a connection with God.

But even that mind set seemed to change when my wife was pregnant, and we had our daughter. As I sat in one of the chairs in the hospital holding my daughter for the first time and reflected on the journey of my wife carrying our child and having her, I thought to myself what a miracle this was. *How can God not exist?* I thought, as I kept holding my daughter and watching her napping peacefully in my arms.

Then another twist. A year after graduate school, I struggled to find work, and my friend referred me to some teaching jobs. I ended up being hired at my first Catholic High School. My plan was to just stay a couple of years and either transition into a different career or to public school because the money and benefits were better. But life happens and I stayed. I would end up staying 10 years at that particular school.

After my first couple of years, my wife would joke with me asking me if I was going to convert. We would laugh it off and just move on, but the longer I stayed the more interested in faith I became. My wife and I tried different services from different faiths and were not the right fit for us. We enjoyed our journey in finding a faith that was right for us.

I then on a whim, started to go to morning masses in the morning before work. Honestly, I went to just be in touch with my spirituality, I had no intention of reverting back to the faith I was baptized in. Over time, a yearning started within me. I would watch people receive communion, and I felt like I am here but missing out on something special. I found myself having discussions about faith with my principal/boss who also happened to be a priest.

Then about two years later when my daughter turned four, I was finishing up grading papers and packing up to leave to go home, and it just suddenly popped into my head, I wanted to revert to the Catholic faith. So, as I walked to the faculty lounge, suddenly felt pulled to the front office, and as if on a spiritual dare I asked if my principal was in, and he was and I told him that I was considering converting and what did I have to do next and he walked me through the process but told me the most important thing is to have an important conversation about it with my wife before I made any decision. I reassured myself that I would but was honestly going to do that anyway. I just wasn't sure how I was going to form the thoughts and words to my wife in my decision. I wanted to reassure her that it was my decision and that she did not in any way have to feel obligated to follow suit. I just wanted her to be supportive of my decision. That is the only thing I wanted. And if she decided to not revert with me, I would be fine with that and I know I needed to support her decision as well, if that was her decision.

All through the drive home, I kept thinking what I was going to say. I pulled into the driveway, and it was about another hour before I was going to pick up our daughter from daycare. My wife was watering the plants. She looked at me and with her girlish optimism while holding the hose, sprayed me quick with the hose and said, "Hi!"

I said hi back and kissed her. I paused.

She could see something was up in my face. "Let me guess, you want to convert and she laughed and kept spraying the plants, as she waited for me to respond.

All the things I wanted to say and thought I wanted to say just went out the window, so I simply said, "Actually yeah."

She stood there looking at me pensive but definitely not in a judgmental way but more out of curiosity than what seemed to be a sudden decision because I did not tell her I was attending mass in the mornings.

But she was very understanding and supportive and said she wanted to take the journey with me, which surprised the hell out of me, as I did not expect that. So, we started slowly by attending Saturday evening masses. Then we started to go on Sundays, and then we signed up for RCIA. For the new generation, it is called the Right of Christian Initiation for Adults. For the older generation, it's catechism.

So we spent six months doing that and on Easter Vigil, the mass that is held the night before Easter, we officially became Catholic and took communion for the first time. It was a beautiful experience. I remember talking to my boss that Monday and he asked me how I felt about coming back to the faith because I was baptized Catholic? I told him I felt like I was coming back home. It was strange and exciting at the same time, this new journey for me and my wife and my daughter.

We ended up baptizing our daughter and raising her in Catholic Schools and she, when she was seven years old, took her first communion. I started to have a good relationship with God again, and this happened.

I then thought about the movie *The Count Of Monte Cristo,* the version with Jim Caviezel. He says he doesn't even know if he believes in God anymore, and the Richard Harris character says, "But God has not stopped believing in you." I thought about that for a minute. Then I whispered to the sky, "I hope you don't give up on me."

CHAPTER EIGHTEEN

I slept through breakfast, group therapy and exercise, but I did get up for lunch. I went to go get my lunch, and my roommate sat across from me. He asked me how I ended up here. I told him that I was confused on what stress caused me to end up here and I was scared that I would never know. He then told me that he attempted suicide. He was telling me why he thought he had to do it, but I focused on the fact that he attempted suicide.

My mind was telling me I should have empathy, especially because he was so open about it. But it just pissed me off, and I got angrier as I thought about what he said, so got up abruptly and cleared my tray. I was going to sit back down but instead I looked at him and said, "That's bullshit. You're a coward and worse, you're selfish."

I walked away and felt bad that I said that. I didn't feel guilty about how I felt, just the way I said it. I walked back to my room and just stayed in bed and stared out the window. My roommate came back into the room after he finished his lunch, so I left and went to the lounge area for a bit.

I watched everyone interacting with different activities. I sat in one of the loveseats and tried to watch TV but just found myself staring out the window. I tried to figure out why I got so pissed. Why did I snap like that? It was because Cookie, in that moment, came into my subconscious.

An Island I Don't Want to Be On

I thought about that time in Puerto Rico about six months before I left the island to go back and live with my dad in California. I do not have fond memories of my time in PR. If I did, it was not enough to count on one hand. That day was pretty normal. I was looking forward to leaving the house. Cookie was in a depressed mood. Her current boyfriend just left her. So, I knew it would be soon that she would start drinking. I didn't want her to, but I knew her moods too well. That depressed mood of hers was brewing, and I knew it was going to throw her in a bad headspace.

I told her I was headed to the river to go swim. She barely looked up at me from her spot by the window, smoking her usual Parliaments, but she did manage to say be back before dark. So I went to the river and had fun swimming and playing rock wars. Looking back, the way we played rock wars, I'm surprised someone didn't get seriously injured or get killed. It was starting to get dark, so I made my way back home. Just as I walked through the front gate it was dark. I found it strange that the porch light wasn't on and didn't see Cookie by the window, drinking or smoking a cigarette, and it was quiet, too quiet. Usually around this time, Cookie has her salsa playing on the radio while she is in the middle of cooking dinner. She played a lot of Hector Lavoe, El Gran Combo, and Oscar DeLeon. She listened to merengue, like Johnny Ventura. I didn't hear any of them. Not hearing the music, not seeing her by the window, the porch light not being on, I kind of got scared.

When I walked through the door, I saw an ashtray with cigarette butts and two empty bottles of Cookie's favorite Cutty Sark. Those green bottles with the yellow label that had a clipper ship on the label, I can't ever forget those images even if I wanted to. Then I heard heavy sobbing coming from the bathroom in the back of the house. I've heard her before in this state, and I would feel so sad and so empathetic. Then, I got used to it and became a little bit numb because eventually I had to help her get into bed.

But this time the sobbing seemed different. I can't quite describe it, but I had never heard her sob like this before. She sounded like a wounded animal. I know that sounds cliche but that is what it sounded like at ten years old. Suddenly the numbness left me and I felt my stomach drop like when you are on a fast ride at an amusement park. I walked in slowly and I saw her holding her arms, wrist first over the sink. I walked closer to the sink and saw a pool of blood.

I yelled, "Mom!"

Chapter Eighteen

She looked up and in her drunken state slurred at me the words, "Where were you?"

I yelled back, "We gotta get you to a hospital."

There was a local bar about four houses down off the rural row we lived on. I rushed over and begged people to help me. All the regulars were looking at me like I was a freak and crazy. They looked at me that way because they didn't want to say what they were really thinking and that is they did not want to help Cookie.

Unfortunately, she was always good at burning bridges. When Cookie left Grandma Carmen's house in New Jersey, we would go and stay at cousins' houses, and eventually Cookie found some way to wear out her welcome. She just could not help herself. She couldn't see the good that our relatives provided us. They gave us a place to say, no questions asked. They fed us, they bought me toys, especially on my birthday and Christmas. I was always grateful and appreciative, but she felt entitled and would get into arguments, then if she didn't get her way, she would yank me out of there, and we would bounce from house to house with different relatives. I remember transferring to three different schools in one year. I always remembered the looks of our cousins when we would leave, like they'd washed their hands of us. I felt sad at that time and even angry, but now I totally understand. I think they did as much as they could to help but they were not willing to sacrifice their own family at Cookie's expense.

These guys in the bar were giving me that same look. Cookie, let me put it in a nice way, dated many of these men, who were all friends with one another. She managed to create a lot of friction. Then at the end of the bar, I saw Pepe. He was a junkyard owner and collector. Out of all the guys she went out with, Pepe was the nicest to me. I would say that he was the closest to being a dad to me than all the other ones, and I was never easily swayed by any of her past men. The rest of them would try to be a disciplinarian and keep me in line, but to Cookie's credit she didn't allow any man to replace my dad. The other half of them just ignored me, which most of the time, was fine with me, unless they wanted to play catch with me once in a while.

But Pepe, he was patient. He would take the time to teach me things, especially when it came to my first love, baseball. He taught me how to grip the ball, how to catch the ball with two hands, how to hold the bat and be in an athletic stance. Even though I sucked at it, he tried to teach me how to fish at the river. I actually liked him ,but Cookie managed to fuck that one up. We were supposed to all go fishing together and make a day out of it. Pepe was going to pack his cooler with ham and cheese sandwiches, beer for him and cookies, and Coke and some candy bars for me. But the night before, Cookie went to some bar on the other side of town, hooked up with some dude, and brought him back to the house. When Pepe showed up, he parked his car and walked toward our hose. Then he saw a different guy's car parked in front of the house, stopped, and started to walk back to his truck. It was weird, like he knew who the car belonged to and he walked away with a purpose.

Despite the bullshit Cookie pulled on Pepe, he came through when I needed him most.

"Pepe, Cookie needs help! She is bleeding everywhere."

I suddenly had this deep feeling that he was not going to help me because he didn't make eye contact with me. Instead, he kept staring at the bubbles in his beer glass and continued to sit there calmly.

"Please, Pepe, I can't let her die!"

He gave me a sad look and then said, "All right, let's go." But he sure didn't rush to get up from his barstool or into his truck.

When we got back to the house and into the bathroom, Cookie looked weak and like she was going to pass out. We wrapped towels around Cookie's wrists and rushed her to the hospital. It seemed like forever until a doctor came in to tell us what was happening. The doctor told us she was lucky; had she used a sharp knife rather than a lid from a tin can she wouldn't have made it. Back then in Puerto Rico, they did not have the medical and mental health services they have now, and looking back I am shocked they released her right away.

After that, I lived in constant fear of leaving her alone. For many years, that guilt weighed on me until I my first go around in therapy and worked out those fucked-up issues.

During my first go around in therapy and working through my depression, that guilt turned into resentment, then anger. Then, I just felt sorry for her that she wanted to waste her life and bring me down with her. Eventually, from an intellectual and I guess psychological standpoint I learned to forgive her in time. I would later understand that her addictions and her inner demons drove a lot of her self-hate and hurt. I do understand that I was also the collateral damage that she did not count on. That is why I was so angry with her in my therapeutic process.

I asked my therapist point blank after Cookie died, "Will I ever forgive her?"

She said, "In time."

She always gave me a gem maxim when things like this came up in our sessions. She said there is a beginning, middle, and end to everything. Your anger with her will someday end. I told her right now I don't forgive her. I don't feel like I ever will. She repeated that I would in time.

I ended up forgiving her but I never forgot and I think that is why I got so pissed off with my roommate. But I realized this guy is not my mom and I had no right to get pissed off at him. I showed no empathy toward this guy. What did he ever do to me for me to react the way I did?

'Nothing,' I said to myself.

Then I got up from the lounge and headed back to the room.

CHAPTER NINETEEN

When I got in the room, he wiggled around in the bed and didn't say anything. I apologized right away. I learned a great lesson in therapy that I always carried with me, and that was you take ownership of your part in a disagreement, apologize, and not try to intellectualize your feelings. Take responsibility over your feelings, and if the other person is open and wants to talk, you share the experience together.

After I apologized, he turned over and made eye contact and just nodded. I then told him the story of Cookie doing what she did and how it affected my life for so many years and in that moment it still affected me. I then told him after I shared that experience that I didn't stop to think what he was going through for him to do what he did. I only thought about what it would do to the people that loved him.

He said, "I know." He covered himself and said, "Don't worry about it."

I did not feel slighted because he turned over. I really felt like he accepted my apology, I just think when I told him how it would affect those that loved him that struck a nerve with him, and I hope I did not strike a hard enough nerve where he is thinking about hurting himself again.

A couple of minutes later, I heard a weird, faint sound. Then I focused my attention on the sound. I then realized my roommate was sawing logs. It sounded like his breathing was louder than his snoring.

I put my head on the pillow and tried to take a nap but was feeling restless. I was really tired still but not as exhausted as I was on my first night here and the next morning.

I decided to walk over to the lounge and occupy myself before dinner. Everyone was doing different activities again, but most people were either playing cards or coloring. Here I am, forty-eight years old and I was thinking about coloring. I can't remember the last time I sat down and colored in a coloring book. I mean the last time was when my daughter was a little kid, but before that, probably when I was eight years old. I know for a fact when I was ten years old and living in Puerto Rico that me or any of the other kids rarely ever colored. We were either playing sports, fighting or stealing something. If anyone in our group mentioned they were coloring, even if they were coloring with a younger brother or sister, would have been laughed at and maybe worse got their ass kicked.

I was hesitant at first, but it reminded me of spending time with our daughter, and I sure was missing the hell out of her, especially since she had a tournament this weekend. In all of her years in sports from the age of four, until now, I had only missed one tournament. It was when I was the head coach of the varsity softball program and she had a big weekend tournament in Vegas. I loved going to her tournaments in Vegas. There was a lot of food, and it was always a blast being there and watching her crush it. I was crushed because we were in a big softball tournament that same weekend.

I was just bummed about missing her tournament. I hoped that she wasn't disappointed that I couldn't make it. I could tell her that I wished I was there rather than here but I knew I had to be here because I want to get better. I'm not good at knowing if I were to leave and go home right now. In my head I understood that but I couldn't reason it with my emotions.

So, I looked at the different coloring books on the table. They had a lot of Disney-themed coloring books, but I picked Kung Fu panda. It was our daughter's first movie we ever took her to, and it was in Vegas. We saw it on a big IMAX screen. At first my wife and I were worried. We didn't know if she was going to sit still and be running around the rows and trying to play hide and seek. She scared the shit out of us two weeks prior when we went to Target. We took our eyes off her for about a split second, and she was gone. We were in a panic for what seemed an eternity, but it was honestly a minute or two before my wife saw a little corner of a foot under a crib in the baby section. It was a daughter's tennis shoe.

Chapter Nineteen

My wife said, "What were you thinking?"

Then she gave her a tight hug and started to tear up. We thought at the movie theater she was going to try to pull the same stunt because she thought it was hilarious hiding from us, but once she got her popcorn and the previews came on the screen, she seemed blown away by the experience, the sound and the images. I never saw her sit still and focus like that before and she ended up being that way through the whole movie. I mean she got into the movie and cheered for Panda and got mad at the characters for not treating him well, but she was so well behaved. From that point, for years to come, it seemed like we were going to the movies every weekend. I mean it was not cheap, but the look on her face and the joy she showed in watching movies was more than worth it.

I grabbed the Kung Fu Panda coloring book and started coloring. I know as a kid I was pretty obsessed when it came to sports or any activity where you had to show skill and I considered coloring a skill. I tried to never color outside the lines. I always did a dark outline on the lines of the object I was about to color. It was like a buffer to keep myself in the lines. It was a pattern. I have always found patterns safe. In a way, I look at it as it keeps my mind from getting destroyed in this current situation. Broken, but not destroyed. So, I decided to keep with the pattern I had as a kid and colored in the lines. As I finished coloring the upper half of the Kung Fu panda, I looked up for a second because the phone rang, but then I went back to my coloring.

Then about twenty seconds later, Tex, an African-American from Texas, walked into the lounge and asked, "Is William here?"

For a split second, I wanted to look behind me for my dad, but I remembered that my insurance information is under my first name. People rarely call me William, but since I have been here, I had been called William more times than I could remember. I wanted to tell them that my name is Hector, but I didn't think they were going to care. They had bigger shit to deal with than to remember to call me by the name I used in my day to day life. And I didn't have the heart to tell the doctors, nurses and staff because they have done a good job, except for the doctor who told me God doesn't exist.

I got up slowly and answered the phone. "Hey Heco, Heco." There was only one person that would ever call me that and that was my dad. My dad had nicknames for all of us Rivera brothers. Mine was Heco, Heco, even though I was two years away from turning fifty. Two years away from being eligible to get an AARP card and here my dad was still calling me by the nickname he gave me in middle school. But, especially in a moment like this, I loved him for it. It was sincere and honest, and I am a sucker for old fashion values like that.

"Hey, Papa! Good to hear your voice."

I always called him Dad until my daughter was old enough to talk and she would call him Papa. Then I would say, "Hey, Papa wants to talk to you. Papa has a gift for you," so Papa stuck. Now I call him Papa all the time.

"Hi you doin my boy?"

I choked back the tears. "I've had better days. I managed to get some good sleep last night. I think it was the first time in years that I got more than eight hours of sleep. I think I slept about 16 hours. I don't think I have ever done that before."

I can't really remember much about the conversation but in the middle of the phone call I went back to 1998.

I remember how stressful the fall semester my first year of graduate school was. Around October, I got a phone call. It was my stepmom. She raised me since I was eleven, so to me, at that point, she was mom. She asked how everything was going. I told her I was just studying and that we were set to have dinner soon. She then asked me if I had any plans after dinner. She told me that she and my dad needed to come over and tell me something very important. I can't really say why, but I didn't ask them why they didn't just save themselves a trip and just tell me over the phone. I think because I was overwhelmed by the first semester of graduate school. I just told them I would be around and hung up the phone and got ready for dinner.

As my then girlfriend was finishing up making dinner, I went in the bathroom and washed up. Then I went to the spare room, which at the time was my study, and turned off the computer. Study-wise, especially because my parents were coming over, I was done for the night. Then I heard a *thud* come from the closet. I looked in the closet and one of my photo albums fell on the floor. When it fell, it seemed like a couple photos fell out. So I picked up the photos and put them back in the photo album. The last one I put back was an old photo of my dad and Cookie on their wedding day. My dad had on a white tuxedo with the black bow tie. He was so skinny then, but he looked good in that tux.

Then I saw Cookie holding her bouquet. They were walking down the steps of the church. What struck me about the photo was how terrified they looked. My dad was nineteen, and Cookie was sixteen. Looking at their faces, they should have never married. But this was a shotgun wedding in 1969. Cookie was pregnant with me. Being Latino in that time period, meant there was just no way that wedding was not going to happen.

After looking at the photo, I put the album back on the upper shelf, and as I left the room, I thought to myself, 'It's been almost three years since the last time I saw Cookie.'

I went back to the dining room and my girlfriend and I had dinner. About forty-five minutes later, I heard a knock at the door.

I walked over to the living room windows facing the front of the house and our street. It was my parents. I noticed what a beautiful fall night it was. As I thought that, a couple of leaves fell down from a tree in the front yard and fell right at my parent's feet. I opened the door.

My mom came through the doorway first and gave me a big hug and a kiss on the cheek, then my dad. Then they greeted my girlfriend in the same way. I led them to the couch and my dad to the love seat because it was like his Lazy Boy at home. Then, I asked them if they wanted anything to drink or eat, and my mom said no thank you but my dad said he didn't mind a glass of water.

So my girlfriend went to the kitchen to get some water for my dad. My stepmom started first with some small talk asking how grad school was and how we liked the neighborhood, as we had just bought the house at the end of summer. I told them how tough grad school was so far, and that I loved the neighborhood, as it was quiet and away from any main street or freeway.

My girlfriend came back with my dad's water and said to my parents that she was going to the bedroom so we could have some privacy, but my stepmom said it was a good idea if she stayed and without hesitation, my girlfriend sat next to me on the sofa.

Once my girlfriend was comfortably seated, my stepmom said, "Hec, we have some bad news."

Instead of asking questions I just sat and waited, but before my stepmom spoke, I took a look at my dad real quick and noticed how pensive he was. He must have known how bad the news was to have my stepmom tell me rather than him. What struck me most about his pensiveness was how sad it was.

Most of the time, my dad tended to be pensive, but this was a pensive look of contemplation. I looked at my stepmom to hear what she had to say.

"Cookie died."

Honestly, I knew this day was coming sooner than later. I hate to say this, but it wasn't a matter of *if* she was going to live a long time. It was a matter of whether she was going to live *long enough* to see that

I had my own family. It was a hope that I didn't believe Cookie would fulfill, and unfortunately on that October evening, I was right.

I imagined how I would feel about that. I mean, I thought years ago if I heard this news, I would be devastated. I remember when after I left Puerto Rico, I did not hear from her until I was around thirteen years old. I did live with her one summer, but that did not work out.

After that, we rarely talked, and I did not hear from her until about seven years later. I honestly thought she was already dead because Grandma Carmen told me that she went back to Puerto Rico. I thought for sure that would be the death knell for Cookie.

Luckily, for a while, it wasn't; even after I heard she was in a love triangle and one of her lovers shot her in the thigh.

Then, out of the blue, I called after I had been out drinking and parting with my homies. I remember just hearing her voice made me emotional. It was that feeling you get when there has been distance created with someone you love, then you get word that they are going to fly into town and you drop whatever you're doing and make plans to go to the airport. That's how I felt when I heard her voice on the phone.

I don't remember much after initially hearing her voice, but I had this fear after I hung up that she was going to die alone, and I became more emotional. I guess that is how I expected to feel when my stepmom told me that Cookie died.

I honestly did not know how to feel other than numb. Not numb from shock. I wasn't shocked to hear that this happened, just numb to what I was supposed to feel because this was the woman who brought me into this world. There were emotions mixing within me but none made sense other than the numbness. Then I noticed my girlfriend holding my hand. She was gripping it tight. That's the *only* thing I remember feeling in that moment - her squeezing my hand.

Momentarily, I felt good because it broke the numbness and for some reason, I looked over at my dad. I saw him wipe away tears. Something inside me started to bubble up.

"Don't cry for her, Dad. She abandoned us. She cheated us. This is bullshit – she cheated me!" Then I looked at my stepmom. "I'm pissed! She cheated me! She didn't even say sorry!"

I just stared at the floor and was really confused. In my experiences of attending funerals and seeing most movies or reading books, when a person hears that their parents have died they are usually sad, morose or even respectful in their demeanor and body language. This was my biological mother and I did not expect to be that angry. It was very rare I would raise my voice at my dad. I immediately looked back at him and said, "Sorry, this is just bullshit. She took the easy way out."

Then after that, it just became small talk. I asked how they found out and where it happened. In honesty, the more we talked about it, Cookie rapidly became irrelevant to me.

For most of the phone conversation that was what I thought about. I then told my dad that I was sorry for getting mad at him when he teared up about Cookie being dead

He told me not to worry about it, that he understood. He told me that he loved me and was proud of me. My dad does not show emotion very much, so I know that was a lot for him. He understood how much Cookie hurt me when I was a kid. I know if he could have, he would have done more. Just the fact that he would fly from California to New Jersey to see me once a month was huge. I knew some of my friends from the neighborhood had dads that only lived two blocks away who wouldn't even acknowledge them as their kids.

He told me that he knew it doesn't make sense now but that Cookie did love me. She just did not know how to show it. I told my dad I loved him very much. I wanted to tell him out loud that if Cookie loved me she would have never left me, she would have not continued with the drugs. I was pissed when he said that – not pissed with him but that her loving me was not believable. But I bit my tongue and told him that I can't wait to see him soon and I hung up the phone and headed back to the lounge.

I went back to the chair with the intention of finishing my coloring, but the thought and memory of Cookie in my head was getting me all worked up, so I decided to go back to my room because I was getting more and more pissed off thinking about Cookie. I wanted to punch and scream in the pillow.

I balled up my fist, ready to punch, and suddenly looked at my daughter's picture on my nightstand. I unballed my fist and a calm came over me. I said to myself, 'I still can't believe I am still pissed at her.' I thought I dealt with a lot of my anger issues with her in my prior therapy years ago.

I was now as confused as I was that day on the sofa in the living room with my parents. I didn't know what was happening to me, but all I could think of was to let go and just be and really think about why did I have such a strong reaction. Maybe I was more pissed off because despite all the hard work in my prior therapy, I still ended up here and I have no idea why. I decided to focus more on trying to make sense of why I was there.

After I got off the phone and went back to the lounge and tried to finish coloring, I was too distracted and kept going back to 1998.

I remember a couple of days after Cookie died I met with my therapist. I shared with her exactly what happened after my parents told me the news. I then asked the question to my therapist: Will I ever forgive her?

I didn't want to hear it at the time, but my therapist said that everything has a beginning, middle and an end. She explained that my anger toward my mother would eventually come to an end.

I told her I didn't want to forgive her. She said she totally understood and that once I process through all of this and do the work to heal what happened to me as a kid, that I would have a better perspective and in time, would forgive her.

Every once in a while, when something like a commercial, baseball game or drug crimes were being reported on the evening news, I would ask myself if I was still pissed at her. Once I asked the question, I could feel a fire starting within me.

I continued to struggle with anger toward Cookie; even after I had left therapy. There was an incident in 2004 when I was at work in the teacher's lounge and conversations about mother's came up. I got agitated and blurted out that I hated my mother. My colleagues thought it was funny because of how quickly I said it. They thought I was being sarcastic, but I told them I wasn't kidding.

Then a year later something changed. I'm not sure what month but Catholic schools have mass once a month. I remember the priest that was leading the mass gave a great homily about forgiveness and how despite Peter denying Christ three times when Christ needed him most, Christ came back and forgave him.

Before mass was over in the concluding prayer, I had a vision of the Virgin Mary, and she was standing in the corner of a dark room. I saw Cookie there. I saw her reaching out to Mother Mary, and before she took her hand, she said to Mother Mary, tell my son I'm sorry for everything I did and she took Cookie by the hand and they disappeared.

I teared up over that and told my wife about it and said, "I think I am starting to forgive my mom, but it still going to take a while."

She said, "It's ok, you take as long as you need to. This is your journey. You don't need to explain it to anyone."

But I couldn't understand why I was still pissed? I thought I forgave her. Then I had a thought – I don't think I'm pissed off at her personally. It's just what she represents: trauma that people go

Chapter Nineteen

through who don't know how to get help or don't have the resources to get help. I think I am still pissed because someone should have helped her. Then maybe she would have had a chance to eventually apologize to me. But we'll never know. After that thought, I rolled over to take a nap before dinner.

When I woke up, I headed to the cafeteria to have dinner. After dinner, I went back to the lounge to watch some TV and my roommate was there. He asked me how I met my wife. I told him he didn't want to hear it, but he insisted.

"Why not?" I said. "We got time anyway."

So I told him. After community college, I transferred to Arizona State. I was interested in becoming a journalist, and they had one of the best programs in the country. I wanted to get out of California for a minute. It was far enough away from home but close enough so I could come home for long weekends and holidays.

I had a shitty first semester. Honestly, I partied too much. I failed every single class except one, in which I got a C. Second semester was better. For some reason, I took a poetry class, and it changed my trajectory. I did really well in the class. I will never forget my professor. She was a Native American woman who was very humble but passionate about poetry. Just before we left for spring break, she pulled me aside and said, "You know, you should pursue poetry. You have a real talent for it."

I was blown away. I have never been told I was talented in something. I felt on top of the world. At that point, I considered changing my major to English and maybe becoming a writer.

So I came home for spring break. I enjoyed my time at home. Then my buddy Frank told me he wanted to go to this club in Redondo Beach called The Strand for their Disco Night.

At first I thought, 'Shit, I fuckin hate disco. This was my last night before I had to go back to Arizona State.'

Then he told me if I went, he'll cover my drinks for the night.

I said ok, and we went.

Then, I heard the band. They sounded familiar. It was this disco cover band called "Boogie Nights." They played at a hot spot called Gibson's in downtown Tempe near Arizona State. They were a fun band and it was a jumpin' club, so I was kind of glad I did go. I even went to the stage and flashed my ASU I.D. and they gave me the thumbs up.

Frank and I walked over to the bar and ordered drinks. I saw a girl I knew named Jenny Jones (like the daytime TV host).

As she walked by, I yelled out to her, "Jenny, Jenny!"

But she didn't respond.

A friend of hers said, "That's not her name," and kept walking.

Frank and I danced with some girls, then went back to the bar.

I saw the girl again. So my stupid ass called out to her again, "Jenny, Jenny!"

And the same girl from before said, (in the way little kids say na-na-na-na) "That's *not* her name."

When she was under the light that was next to the bar, I could see her face. She was glamorous with a way about her.

"She looks like my friend Jenny from high school," I said.

"Clearly she's not," said the girl and laughed a little.

"I guess not," I said.

I introduced myself and asked her name. She told me. I noted how tall she was. She was about 5-10. She had a model look but not as waify and skinny looking. She had a great pair of legs. The more I talked to her, the more she was sexy to me, in a very subtle way. I finally came around and asked her to dance.

At the end of the night, she gave me her number and said she heard that the Gypsy Kings were having a concert in Phoenix soon and that maybe we should go. I said it sounded like a plan.

We didn't make the concert, but once the semester was done and I came home that summer, we spent time together for a bit. I could see things were working out the more we talked and the few times we saw each other.

A lot of it was because I was struggling hard with my depression at that time. I would, especially if we went to a club and drank, poor my heart out to her and reveal all of who I was. At the time, I didn't understand the concept of taking things slow or getting to develop a relationship. I would tell her stories about my mom. At one point I think it was too much for her and she told me I should see someone and that she wasn't built to take on what I was telling her. I got pissed and slammed the phone.

From that point, I didn't really contact her much unless I was drunk or horny, but that seemed to not ever work.

At that time, I was obsessed with watching a late night show that was wildly popular called *The Jerry Springer Show*. It was hosted by the former mayor of Cincinnati. He was also a city council member but resigned because he hired a prostitute. I would tell her about the episodes. It seemed every episode the guests would get into a full-blown brawl and melee that bordered on a riot. She didn't seem to care much about the show and thought I was wasting my nights.

About a year later, I had my first breakdown and started to go to therapy. I started to really work hard on my issues. Later that year, I moved out of my parents' house and in with my buddy Frank. I decided to call her one night and asked her if she wanted to play pool sometime.

She blew me off. She even said, "Play pool?" in a very sarcastic way. So I wished her good night and hung up.

About three months later, I decided to give it one more shot and left a message. A couple of weeks later, Frank moved out. I couldn't find a roommate in time so I had to move back in with my parents temporarily.

Then, I got a phone call. It was her. She said that she was in Cancun for a month and when she returned, she heard my message.

She was up late one night and decided to watch an episode of *The Jerry Springer Show*. After the episode, she called me at the old apartment only to discover that my old number was disconnected. She then took a chance and called me at my parents and she got a hold of me. She asked me what I was up to lately, I told her I was a few months from graduating.

I also told her that I had started seeing a therapist and it helped me to deal with the issues I was always sharing with her. We talked for an hour and then, to my surprise, she asked me if I wanted to get together for dinner.

I said, "Yeah, that would be cool."

We went and had a great time. Then she invited me to her friend's wedding where she was going to be a bridesmaid. After that wedding, we seemed to really click. The rest is history. We have been married ever since. That was 21 years ago – 21 together, 17 married.

He looked at me and said, "That's a cool story. I hope to have something like that for me." But he said it with sadness.

"You will," I said despite his sadness. "I never expected to get married. My stepmom was worried about me and asked when I was going to bring a nice girl home? I told her that I will give myself until I'm forty. If I don't, I'm going to be like Hugh Hefner and travel the world having as much sex as I can with beautiful foreign women."

My roommate laughed a little.

To cheer him up even more, I told him about the wedding speech and how, when I was nearing the end of my first semester in graduate school, I was becoming incredibly stressed. When my future wife came home, she saw how stressed out I was. She came out to the back patio and saw all these books I checked out of the library with a ton of notes on the patio table. I told her this was a lot and that I needed to go for a drive.

When I got back, the house was very quiet. I even called out to her but no answer. I looked all around the house - nothing. Then, I went to the back patio, there she was combing through the different books with a yellow legal pad. I didn't say anything at first, I just watched her take notes. It nearly brought me to tears.

I said to myself, "She really loves me."

It reminded me of a scene from *Wyatt Earp* with Kevin Costner. In the movie scene, Wyatt's girlfriend, Josie, tells him to give her a gun and that she would kill anyone who tried to hurt him.

When I saw that scene, I said, "That is the type of woman I will marry." When I saw my future wife going through those books, she was my Josie.

When I was done telling him the story, he smirked and said, "*Wyatt Earp*, hmm?"

I sort of laughed too and said it was the truth and I was sticking to it.

After I shared that story, we watched the NBA on ESPN. I saw a commercial about some upcoming MLS soccer game. I started thinking about my dad and his phone call and how he told me he loved me and was proud of me, and I started really appreciating that, especially, because it was a rough road for a while in my teens and in college.

When I was eleven and I first came back from Puerto Rico, I didn't realize at the time, I was a mess. I had forgotten quite a bit of English. Within a week, I was enrolled in school I got into a fight almost every day because the kids were making fun of me because I was struggling with my English. I pretty much struggled with everything.

I lacked respect, I lacked discipline, and my dad was tough on me about it. And at the time, I really struggled with the structure he and my stepmom were trying to provide for me. I wasn't used to being called in from being outside playing at dusk. I didn't like having to go to bed at 9 p.m. every night. I didn't like having to eat everything on my plate in order to be excused from the table.

I always wondered why he was so strict and tough on me. I think it had to do with how tough a kid I was. I was fragile emotionally as far as following directions and being focused in school and doing chores. But I was tough when it came to sports or fighting.

Chapter Nineteen

We just had trouble connecting, and for many years I didn't understand it. My dad had trouble communicating to me what he expected in a supportive and positive way, and I had trouble accepting the structure and environment that was going to help me succeed.

There were moments, where honestly he made what I perceived to be mean comments, at least as far as tone was concerned. He was not abusive or cold blooded in his expressions of frustrations. I was crushed several times by his timing and tone. I remember in sixth grade I got all A's on my report card but I had one C. I just struggled with math. It's like a foreign language to me. I just wanted him to be proud of me. It is the hardest I had ever worked in school. All he said was, "but you got a C in math." I waited until I got to my room and I cried.

As I was finishing up community college, I brought home some applications to fill out to schools I was interested in attending. He looked at the applications and said, "With your GPA how do you think you are going to get into any of these colleges?"

It was weird, I thought I was going to be pissed off as hell, but I went to my room and I am a grown man at this point, and I cried and felt almost exactly the same as I did in 7th grade.

Then it happened again when I came back home after I attended one year at Arizona State. I told him that I did not do well my first semester and that I was put on academic probation, and as part of the probation that I would have to stay and attend summer school. The combination of changing my major and having to pay for summer school was just too much for me, so I wanted to transfer to Long Beach State to save money. He just nodded and said, "See, I knew it," and walked out of the room.

In some weird way, I knew he loved me and I loved him, but we just could not seem to tell or show each other that we did. Even though he hurt me in the things he *said*, I know that I hurt him in the things I *did*.

I never told him how I appreciated him for helping me get out of the situation with Cookie. I feel, at a subconscious level, that I had a sense of entitlement with him from the things I suffered with while I was with Cookie. I was always talking back to my stepmom and complained when my dad would want me to do chores on the weekend. On the day of prom, when he paid for everything for me to go and all I had to do was my chores and clean my room as a thank you to him, I didn't.

But our relationship had started to change. My dad had brought my grandpa and grandma from Peru because my grandpa was starting to have major health problems, and my dad knew that he would get better healthcare in the states. They lived with us for a while until about the middle of high school when they were able to get an apartment several blocks from us.

Once I got my car, I would help them out with groceries and take them to wherever they needed to go when my dad wasn't available. Once I got to college, my grandpa's health worsened. His diabetes was causing his kidneys to not function properly, so he had to start going to dialysis. I took him in between classes then picked him up afterwards.

One day I was about to go pick him up and saw an ambulance in front of their apartment. Then someone brought out a gurney, wheeling my grandpa off. He was writhing in pain. I asked my grandma what happened. She said he had a really bad fall in the living room. So, I called my dad and told him what happened and that I was going to follow the ambulance to the hospital.

They gave him pain medication that made him loopy and said he was seeing ants walking on the walls. But I knew something was wrong. I could see it through his eyes. As the day went on, his condition worsened, and later in the early evening he passed. My uncle was there with my dad next to grandpa's bed. They then suddenly both started crying. It was the damndest shock to me. I never saw my dad even sad or scared, but there he was crying. I just wasn't expecting that.

A week later we had a viewing for grandpa before shipping his body back to Peru to be buried in the family cemetery. I watched different people walk to the open casket and pay their respects. Then, I saw my dad go up. I was sitting off to the side and could see his profile. As he stood over the casket, he looked so lost. You could tell that there was a lot of unfinished business between my dad and my grandpa. I just kept looking at my dad hoping I would not be in the same situation.

After my grandpa returned to Peru, it seemed that things slowly but surely got better. About a year later was when I first went to therapy. My dad approached me with a curiosity about therapy. After about six months, he asked me if it was helping. I told him yes, it was helping me a lot. I told my therapist about it, and she suggested to me to see if he wanted to have a joint session.

My dad and I went for our joint session, and I could tell he was very nervous, but once we had our session he really opened up in a way I did not expect. I thought he may get defensive or want to leave. It turned out that after that session he went to see Dr. Westfield on his own and I could tell it really helped him.

Every year after that, we became a little closer and things really went into a different direction once our daughter was born. When he held his grandaughter, I saw such tenderness in him that I really connected to. I imagine that is how he felt the first time he held me.

He held her and said, "I'm very proud of you, my son."

After he and my stepmom left, I sat on the chair and my wife looked at me and asked, "Are you ok?"

I said, "Maybe he said it before and never heard him, but that is the first time I ever heard my dad say he was proud of me."

And our relationship hasn't looked back since. So his phone call to me while I was in that place meant even more to me.

CHAPTER TWENTY

I snapped out of that moment when I was called over to take my medication. I thought about how I had a good life. I thought about the story of my wife and how good my dad and I were since the birth of our daughter and couldn't wait to see them and everyone once I got out of there.

After I took my medication, I sat back down, and watched some more TV. It was the first time I felt whole since I was there. For a moment, I didn't seem so out of control and lost and faithless. I tried not to overthink it and just let this feeling be, but I couldn't. I fulfilled my own promise of not ending up like Cookie and other family members on her side of the family. I'm a good husband, a good dad, a good son, a good brother but I still ended up here. How did I let it get to this point? Yes. It was my choice to be here because I know I needed to get better and I know I can't do this on my own, but I just became so confused now with all of this.

One of the staff members said the doctor wanted to see me and guided me to the office. I was so relieved when I saw it was a different psychiatrist. She interviewed me extensively. She was concerned at first because of my interview with the prior psychiatrist who thought I was bipolar. She said she didn't think that I had bipolar disorder, that it was most likely I had an anxiety disorder.

"So I am not going insane?" I asked her.

"No," she said, "you're not. It was most likely caused by an overwhelming amount of stress. That is why I am confused. This was the one breakdown that I had that I can't pinpoint what triggered it. I noticed you missed every group session in the mornings."

I said yes.

"Maybe it will be a good idea to go to a group," she said.

I told her thank you and that I would think about it and left her office and felt a little less confused than I did when I went in.

As I got back to my room, I saw that they gave my roommate his things. He was packing up. I was happy for him, but I worried about him. I asked him if he was going to be okay and he just nodded. I noticed he looked relieved but a little sad still, but that was understandable. I don't know anyone that wouldn't have conflicted emotions being in his situation.

I told him to hold on a minute, and I ran over to a staff member and asked them to write my phone number down. I came running back with the small piece of paper I gave him my phone number.

I then reached out to shake his hand and told him if he needs someone to talk to give me a call. Instead of shaking my hand, he gave me a quiet but warm hug. As he was about to walk out, he turned to say, "Hearing about you and your wife…it gives me hope," and he quickly left the room before he could get emotional in front of me.

I started to tear up. I was still a little worried but just hearing hope come out of his mouth gave me some relief and temporary distraction from my own shit. At the same time, him saying that opened a glimmer of hope in me I hadn't felt in a day and half. Up to this point, I was just surviving, existing. I got a little jolt of energy from processing what my roommate said and my emotions that were surfacing. It gave me hope.

The minute I stepped in here, I thought I was going insane, and would ask staff members, psychiatrist, nurses, anyone willing to listen, "Am I going insane?"

They all said the same thing - "No," or "No, I have seen worse."

I now was filled with a grain of hope that they were right, and that they were not just blowing smoke so I would calm down or shut up. Even at this moment, I felt like I was not losing my mind or that I would be locked up here for longer than seventy-two hours.

After my roommate left, I headed back to the lounge. The male nurse that first admitted me was supervising the lounge. I would love to tell you the name of the male nurse and many of the staff members because they were so supportive and helpful, but I have always been

bad with names. Faces I never forget. I'm also good at recognizing peo
I then saw the lady psychiatrist walking with my old roommate.

I then saw the lady psychiatrist walking with my old roommate.

He was being relieved by another staff member. I felt uneasy, so I got up and followed them into the hallway but was careful in my approach because I didn't want either of them to think I was stalking. I asked the lady psychiatrist if we could talk. I told her that my roommate just left. And that all of a sudden I was scared.

"Why are you scared?"

"I'm scared that I am leaving tomorrow and I don't know what is going to be out there for me when I'm released."

I paused.

"It's too much to unload right now. I'm sorry. It was a mistake to do this. You are probably on your way home ready to get to your life away from work."

I tried to walk away, but she gently put her hand on my shoulder and said, "It's fine. It can wait."

I shared with her that I was feeling the same fear that I felt when my biological mother almost killed herself. That I felt like that scared little kid that didn't know what is going to happen next.

She said, "I know you are going to be all right."

I was so struck with her confidence that I had to ask, "How do you know?"

She said, "I've seen the picture of your daughter that you carry around with you most of the time. The smile on her face and how she has never seen the things you have seen. And she probably won't. You are a big part of that. You are going to be all right because you are going to be there when she continues to smile like that."

I paused and thought about that.

Wow. That's the only thing I could think of and I say that in an almost peaceful and joyful way. It was the first time in three days, where my mind paused completely for an extended amount of time. My mind was quiet. My mind was empty. It felt like a first step back to normalcy. My mind was speechless, and for a bit, I just took it in and enjoyed it; something I haven't done for a while, even before landing there. I thought about how I felt when I was holding our daughter. This is how my mind felt. In such awe that it quieted my mind and that is a place where you find joy and peace. Though that is fleeting, it's always good to feel that way, even if it is for thirty seconds in your life.

An Island I Don't Want to Be On

I picked up my daughter's photo and thought about the day we went for the wife's ultrasound and the doctor telling us we were going to have a girl. Outside of marrying my wife, I had never felt so much joy. I then thought about Cookie. I thought about what it was like for her before I was born.

Did she even experience one third of what I felt? Then I thought about all the painful moments Cookie had shared with me when she went on her drunk benders. It seemed to always happen when it was her father's birthday or the anniversary of his death, or my Grandma Carmen's birthday. I thought about a picture my aunt gave me after Cookie's death. It was a picture of Cookie and my dad walking down the church steps on their wedding day. On the back it said, "This was when Cookie was nice."

But when I looked at the photo, her and my dad looked terrified. They were teens. They didn't know what they were doing. They were kids themselves. It didn't seem in any way that once I was born she could have felt the same joy I had as a new dad. If she did, it was probably momentarily. But I wasn't sure. At least that was what was in my mind, and I could never be in hers. But I would never have that chance to ever talk to her about it.

But I did realize something. Despite everything, she would have enjoyed our daughter, because I remember our daughter once said, after looking at some old photos and home movies of me growing up with Cookie, that she would have liked to have met Cookie. I was so struck by that. It was like Cookie communicating with our daughter. I did not know what to say to our daughter other than just look at her in a way that she filled me with love and joy because of the goodness in how she said that.

And despite my past difficulties with Cookie, I would have not denied our daughter that opportunity because I know it would put a smile on both of their faces.

I started thinking about my stepmom and the difficult times I had with her. I was such a little prick to her. When I would come over for summer visits from New Jersey, I know I made an effort every day to tell her or remind her that she couldn't tell me what to do because she was not my mother. Even when I felt she was being nice to me and I wanted in some way to acknowledge her for it, I would find a way to tell her my mom doesn't do that or "You'll never do it like my mom did."

I remember she would tell me it was nap time, and many times I would fight tooth and nail and my dad would remind me in a very definitive and firm way that I better take those naps or "you gonna find out what's good for you."

So I gave in. I remember she was sitting next to me and she, out of nowhere, noticed I was slowly falling asleep. But I was fighting it, so she started to rub my head. It felt so good and for a moment, I remember wishing that Cookie would have done that for me and something kind of snapped within me.

I told my stepmom, "I hate naps," and I just sat up.

Eventually, I slept sitting up because, even though I like the gentleness that she showed me, I felt like my stepmom was helping me betray Cookie. I just could not bring myself to do that to Cookie.

But eventually, as the years passed and I completed high school and college, that feeling that I was betraying Cookie would disappear.

CHAPTER TWENTY-ONE

It must have been divine intervention or something because as I flashed back to that moment a staff member knocked on my door and told me I had a phone call. It was my stepmom. We talked for a while. I told her that "The worst thing in life is to leave things unsaid to those who mean the most to you. I wanted to say sorry for all the things I put her through. And that Cookie may have given me birth and carry the title of my mother on my birth certificate but she is my mom, and I love her very much for everything she did for me in this life." We both cried on the phone together. At the end of the phone call, I told her "I love you, Mom."

After the phone call with her, I was on the fence whether I wanted to go back to my room or the lounge. I had about an hour left before lights out. I didn't want to back to the room because I was ready to pour out my emotions and I knew I would be alone in my room afterwards, so I didn't want to do that, but I knew the other patients or staff members were going to see me emotional and I didn't really want to talk about it.

I decided to stay in the lounge, but the longer I stayed the more uneasy I felt. I started to think more and more about my breakdown. What caused it? Does it really matter to dwell on it when it's not going to matter when I get out of here. But that is my downfall. I overanalyze things because I don't like the unknown. I don't like a future that doesn't seem to have at least a hint of an answer. The fear of the future and of the unknown, based on my past traumas, maybe it has always been there. But my being conscious about it started when I quit playing football in collage at the start of my sophomore year.

All I ever wanted to be was a professional athlete and once I hit high school, I had big dreams of making it to the NFL even though, realistically, I lacked the physical size to even land a Division 1 scholarship out of high school. Still, I loved football so much that I at least wanted to die trying. I at least had a good first season, despite being solely a special teamer. I was even a player of the week as a special teamer, and I had more tackles on special teams than some of the starters and guys who got more playing time than me. I had a great bowl game at the season end, so I was hyped, looking forward to my sophomore year. But I suddenly was not on as many of the special teams that I used to be on. The year before I was on three teams – kickoff, kickoff return, and punt team. Suddenly, without even playing one game, the coaches only put me on one team, kickoff. As disappointing as it was, I still held out hope.

Then, I decided to approach my defensive coordinator to ask him if there was any chance if I worked hard enough that I could get more playing time. He then explained to me that we are one of the top community college football teams in the nation, that he didn't really see me getting much playing time. I sat on the bench where we were talking and I was devastated, like someone in my family died. He tried to comfort me, and he hugged me and said he loved that I worked my ass off. But I didn't even know how to process that. It hit me so hard.

That was an excruciating lesson about fairness. What I ended up learning was some primadonna malcontent, who mouths off to his coaches, misses half the practices in a week, or only goes to half of his classes, he was still going to be a starter or get significant playing time.

Your work ethic, your discipline, your knowledge of the game and consistency of attending class did not matter. In that moment I learned the hard way that fairness was mythical and bullshit.

I was contemplating quitting after that point. My closest teammates were day after day convincing me not to do it. So I hung in thinking, 'even though I may not play very much, I may have a chance to win a national championship ring, and still hang with my teammates.'

But we lost the very first game at home, and that was really unexpected. Then, we lost the next week as well. I already started to lose my love for football. And then I did not want anything to do

Chapter Twenty-One

with it. It left a bad taste in my mouth. I wasn't having any fun at all. It was a job now that I was growing to hate, and if I stayed on, I was going to hate it more and be a distraction to the team. So, I decided to quit. I cried about it that night, but I felt relieved like a burden was lifted off my shoulders. It went against everything I learned in playing sports about not quitting and perseverance but that mindset was warped and destroyed from the beginning of that season.

My mindset then became that my education was more important than football or sports in general. That was in 1990 when all that happened. I honestly did not follow or watch a single sports event, at least not in its entirety. I wasn't even watching Sports Center on ESPN at all. Not until 1996 when my beloved Yankees made it to the World Series and won. That's when I fell back in love with baseball and my Yankees again.

But after I quit, I was really lost. Even though I knew how important education would be going forward, I had no idea what I wanted to do. I knew it was important to finish college. I knew I definitely wanted to do that, but to finish what. I bounced around some majors, starting with fire science because I thought I wanted to be a firefighter. Then, I majored in journalism because I thought at first I wanted to be a sportswriter because I was very knowledgeable about sports. Plus, I heard an advertisement about how sports media was a multibillion dollar industry and how easy it was to get in. In reality it wasn't, plus, I started to develop an interest in writing beyond sports stories.

Despite that, I still felt lost. I was terrified of what I was going to be. I masked that fear with a lot of partying. Yeah, I was getting my credits done and trying to graduate but I did take my sweet ass time getting to the finish line. And I finally did finish and eventually went on to get my Master's Degree.

Up to this point had a nineteen-year career as a teacher and coach, but right then I was scared to know where to go. This fear took me to that place after I quit football. I felt lost and that scared the shit out of me to think I may go through that again, and it scared me more while in this voluntary hold because I had a family and I didn't want to let them down.

Maybe that is what caused my breakdown, a need for an answer to things. Despite knowing details of the trauma my mother put me through, I still don't and won't ever know what motivated her to do the things she did. Yes, I can describe her trauma and dysfunction, but I don't know what was in her heart and in her head other than she beat herself up a lot through her addictions. I recognize now she carried a lot of guilt and feelings of worthlessness. Maybe I will never know what caused this last panic attack. I have to learn to just be and find my peace with myself and know at this point it doesn't really matter in the whole scheme of things.

I had returned to my room and settled into my bed. I stared out of my window at the L.A. skyline and decided that it was not going to do me any good to overanalyze how I got here. So I decided to go to sleep and just head into tomorrow doing the best I could because I would be leaving in two days.

CHAPTER TWENTY-TWO

The staff nurse came in and announced that breakfast is ready. In the days I have been here, I slept in and missed breakfast every single day. I decided I will have it today. I headed over to breakfast and quietly ate.

'One more day,' I thought to myself, 'one more day.'

I went back to my room and rested in bed thinking about my breakdown that landed me here. I just didn't want to leave here without having some idea or theory of what happened to me. I started to think simplistically, almost mathematically even though it went against my nature as an English teacher. My breakdown this time around happened while I was in the classroom. Did that have anything to do with it? I started to reflect on my teaching career.

All these thoughts, people, students, my coaching staff when I coached all flashed in my head, and my head felt like it was spinning. I could feel my heart beat a bit faster.

I closed my eyes and attempted to slow everything down and slowly everything did calm me down. I went back to the beginning.

The more I reflected, the more I slowed down and decided to go back to the beginning and reflect on my first teaching job because maybe it could unlock what happened days ago in that classroom.

After graduating with my Masters, I thought it would be easy to find a job but struggled for the first three months. It was not because of a lack of effort. I bounced around from interview to interview. I finally landed a job as a bilingual editor and was fired after a week because I lacked the Spanish writing skills to keep the job. I was devastated and embarrassed.

After about another month of editing, I landed a new job working as an editor for a health insurance company. That job sucked from the beginning. I was supposed to take over for this guy who was going to travel around the world, and he asked me to come in for his last week so he could train me, but he didn't at all. I sat in an empty cubicle just reading my book of short stories by Raymond Carver. It was a temporary job through an agency, and after three months I was laid off. Then a friend of mine from graduate school called me and asked if I needed a job. It was a job to tutor Korean kids at a learning center in Orange County. I thought I was going to hate it, but it was pretty cool. I thought that the tutoring job was seasonal and they were going to shut down for the summer. I was worried about how I was going to make money when my girlfriend and I were set to get married the following summer.

My girlfriend encouraged me to fill out applications for teaching jobs and take a temporary teaching job until I found another writing or editing job. So, I applied for a couple of teaching jobs and about a week later, I got a call for a job interview. Honestly, I did not put a lot of effort and heart in the interview. I was just trying to get through the interviews and looked at it as a temporary situation.

I remember one interview was for a Catholic School. I just gave really short answers because I had a lunch date with my girlfriend that I didn't want to be late for. Plus, the principal was a priest and I was agnostic at the time and had no interest.

But I then got a call a couple of days later from that same principal. I told the principal/priest, knowing in the back of my head it would only be temporary, I said, "Yeah, I guess I will take the job." He sounded more excited about me taking the job then me finally having a job where I could soon start paying off my student loans and save some money for our wedding next summer.

I was talking to my dad about accepting the teacher job. My dad is an accountant, and he suggested I meet with a teacher client of his to prepare for the job. His client/teacher recently retired after 30 years in the Los Angeles Unified School District. Before meeting with him, I had visions of how my first day was going to go. I thought that I was going to be like Robin Williams in the movie *Dead Poets Society*, that I was going to shape and inspire young minds, that I was instantly

Chapter Twenty-Two

going to change the world, but when I met with the retired teacher I was in for a rude awakening.

He told me how I needed to be. How I needed to go in there and set the tone and establish seating charts and go over the rules of the class and school even before I even taught my first lesson.

He told me yes, care about the students, connect them to the work, but most important if you want them to respect you and you want them to succeed, he suggested to not smile until Christmas.

I was like, "Shit what did I sign up for?"

I don't get intimidated easily by anyone or any situation, but after that meeting with my dad's client, I was overwhelmed. He walked me to his front door. He assured me, if I set the tone early and often, that I would succeed. If I didn't then I would suffer burn out and would be out of teaching in three years. I wanted to succeed, yes, but he didn't realize that I wasn't planning to stay that long.

My first day on the job went smooth for the most part. The students looked intimidated but attentive. Also, I had a class full of seniors for journalism that I would be teaching in addition to my four freshman English classes. The seniors were ok but not as intimidated as the freshman. I was not going to get away with not smiling until Christmas with the seniors, but I was going to at least try in order for them not to get out of hand and develop an early case of senioritis.

One senior, as I was walking down the aisles to check students' work, told me to "keep my booty out of her face." I was embarrassed I didn't know I was so close in between the rows. Another senior raised his hand and asked if any of the discipline I was implementing was going to work.

I found out pretty quick what this job was really about the next day. I assigned a couple of chapters to the students to read for homework the previous night. I opened it up to a class discussion. For a few moments, it was dead silence. Then I had a brave soul raise his hand and when I called on him, he asked if he could go to the bathroom. The next one a few moments later asked for some tissue and another one to sharpen their pencil and that one pissed me off the most because the rule of thumb in an English class is to use blue or black ink, not pencil.

After the first couple of weeks, I was so exhausted I would fall asleep early. As the days and months of the semester passed, things were pretty much this way. I learned before Christmas that I didn't smile and they somewhat learned, but that there is a rule of threes when it comes to teaching. About a third of the students you don't have to talk too much, just guide them in the right directions; and you don't have to hold their hands too much. Another third of them want to disrupt and do as little as possible in the class just to keep themselves from getting bored; they are not bad kids; just fell through the cracks of learning how to make good decisions and being self-disciplined and self-motivated to pursue their potential. The last third was trying to figure out which third they want to be a part of.

I wanted to get more kids to move their way into that first third, but I knew I couldn't control that. All I could do was the best I could. Over time, things got better. I felt like I was getting through to the students. I still wasn't sure if I wanted to come back to teaching; though there were very rewarding moments, I still wanted a writing or editing job.

At the school's graduation ceremony, I was announced as the best new teacher recipient. Honestly, I was really shocked. But I was incredibly grateful and thankful because I know the students, not the administration, were the ones that voted for that award, and there were five new teachers that year and I knew they were motivated. I was trying to make the most of my situation until I moved on to another job that I wanted. But, no interviews were in sight for my immediate future, so if I could not find a writing job over the summer, I decided to give teaching one more year.

Not only did I stay that year in my first teaching job, but I would go on to stay for nine more years at this particular school. As a teacher, I had some incredible moments, but our school leadership had changed. Two years prior, our principal, the priest who hired me, was promoted for another assignment.

I knew the two people he was going to put in charge. As a matter of fact, one of them was my daughter's godfather. We came in together and became great friends. I had a hard time adjusting to the leadership though. It was confusing at first. We all were told about the new principal. My old principal, over the past five years, had wanted me to be his replacement. But rumor had it that my good friend and my old principal had a conflict over the decision. Then, last thing I knew, my good friend became the principal.

I thought that with my buddy as principal, that the transition would be very smooth. His principles and vision did not vary from my former principal. At least at first that's how I felt, but after two years things seemed to change. I mean, I expected some differences, some changes, but it just started to really change a lot. I remember in the middle of the meeting my buddy went off on the faculty about a lot of

Chapter Twenty-Two

things that had nothing to do with curriculum or learning or the day to day operations of the school. He was going off about the parents and how the faculty does not do small things like turn off the lights in the bathrooms or keep the lounge clean. I understood his frustration, but it was expressed in an unprofessional tone and manner – definitely in tone because he was supposed to be our leader and principal yet was talking to us like we were a bunch of football players.

Finally, one of the teachers I most respected spoke up. This was my ninth year, and this faculty member was there about ten years before me. She basically told him that he should not be talking to us in that manner, that we should be focusing on academics and how to help the students learn or how to make us better teachers.

He got heated after that and was very defensive, and I was really pissed off at this point because this is one faculty member he should have been listening to. That is when I spoke up and told him out of all the people here she was one person that does not deserve to be spoken to like that, that he needed to check himself and have more restraint and self-control, that if he had a problem with some of things that were going on that he needed to find out who specifically is the problem and address them individually instead of going off on us in a meeting and especially going off on a great resource such as our respected faculty member. I told him it would take a lot for her to say anything and that he needed to be wiser to recognize something is not right if she is speaking up.

I know I was being dramatic, but I was willing to die on the hill for her. Plus, it was also my way of saying that he and the president were not keeping the model and the principles that our former principal established that made our school great. Once that teacher spoke up, I had had it with biting my tongue.

I was heated by the end of the meeting. I knew I had enough leverage and nothing to lose at that point, despite him and the new president getting rid of some teachers already. So he asked me if we could talk. I told him "Hell no" and continued to my class to get ready for the school day. I noticed he followed me to my classroom and followed me in.

"Come on, let's talk," he said.

I told him "Fuck you, I don't want to talk."

"Come on man."

"No. What you did was bullshit, and you know our former principal would never do that. He always handled things individually. All this shit you brought up was petty, and taking it out on that specific faculty member was way out of line. You need to check yourself and reassess how you are doing your job because this is not the way to do it." Then I told him I was done and need to get ready for class.

I wish I could say that things would get better, but they didn't. It got progressively worse. I could tell, for the first time in my career, that I was losing my motivation. That teaching was becoming a pain in the ass job that I had to pay my bills. The students were becoming annoying.

I was just trying to get through my days. I remember there was one student who found a sneaky way to listen to headphones in the back corner during class. I wasn't keeping up with upholding uniform monitoring and some kids had taken to wearing their hoodies in class with earphones in. I then heard rumoring from students of mine that the vice principal was basically spying on me at an angle of the hallway through the little window within the door of my classroom. But he was at an angle where I could not see him. I don't mind if an administrator wants to come in and observe my class. I have nothing to hide, but I thought it was bullshit and petty, and he wasn't coming around at all until my new principal, my good friend, probably told him to start doing that.

So, one day, I guess the vice principal noticed one too many times that this student was consistently wearing a hoodie with her headphones and I obviously did not catch it. So, he opened my door and asked to see me in the hallway. He then told me he has been observing my class and that every time he has observed from the window, she had her headphones on.

I told him ok, that I will try to monitor it. And I did for about a week and just forgot about it. He then, a week later, knocks on my door again, and calls me to the hallway. I told him straight up that I didn't appreciate how he was handling this. I told him that I didn't have a problem being observed but it would be more professional to just come into my class. And that it would also be more professional if instead of pulling me into the hallway, he set up a meeting with me to discuss the issue..

Of course, he kept observing me through the window and decided to call me in for a meeting. Instead of being supportive and saying that he had strategies that could help me deal with this situation, he basically took what said to him and threw it back in my face.

It wasn't what he said, it was *how* he was saying that rubbed me the wrong way.

I let him go on and on, and finally just said, "Are we done? This is taking up way too much of my lunch break," and I just left.

But I think what was the low point was when my buddy approached me about teaching a seventh period class. A seventh period is typically held before and/or after school and the rationale is for students to be able to have school time to work on and complete their activities no later than 4pm. This is a dream scenario for athletics, but it does benefit drama and music programs as well.

To teach seventh period is strictly voluntary, and you get a stipend for it. I was helping with building the golf program but was not interested in coaching it. I just wanted to be like an athletic director for the golf program as far as setting up golf courses, finding coaches for the boys and girls programs, setting up clinics, finding sponsors and donors for golf equipment. My daughter was very young at the time, and I was not interested in sacrificing that time to coach. I wanted that seventh period time to class prep and deal strictly with building the golf program.

So, out of desperation, my principal buddy basically begged me to take a seventh period study hall class. Being a former football coach and former athletic director, he needed a study hall for football players who were in danger of being ineligible for the following fall season. I knew what he was attempting to do. I told him that I would do it under two conditions. The first was that the majority of kids are golfers. The second condition was that the class size does not exceed twelve kids. He agreed.

However, a week later, I suddenly had twenty-seven kids, the majority of them football and basketball players. I was pissed. I sent a note
with one of the golfers to ask one of the counselors who was a close friend of mine to come to my class and please explain to me what was going on.

About ten minutes later, she came to my door. The only reason I requested her was because my principal and president were coincidentally unavailable.

I went into the hallway and said this was bullshit and that I was tired of their bullshit decisions. I felt bad, I got caught up in the moment, and I raised my voice about my grievances with the administration. The problem was when I was expressing myself to her I used several curse words and there happened to be other students and faculty in the hallway.

Naturally, I got called into the office by my buddy the principal. He, of course, read me the riot act saying he didn't have to explain or justify putting all those kids in my class.

I reminded him we had an agreement and that I never wanted to take a seventh period class. We were going round and round, and he at one point just stopped and pulled out what is called a counseling notice. It is basically saying you are being written up and states what you have been written up for, then you have sign it. I was really tempted not to sign it, but a moment of calm came over me, and I thought, 'I have a family to provide for and I can't jeopardize that.' So, I calmly signed the damn paper and walked out.

Several months later, out of the blue, he approached me with an opportunity. He, along with our school president, were now running two schools. Because of the economy, quite a bit of Catholic schools were shutting down. There was a school about thirty minutes away with the same leadership and curriculum. The principal and the president later told us this news at a faculty meeting. They also told us that there would be new teaching positions opening at the school and that if any of us wanted to change or have a shorter commute, we could transition into working at the other school.

So after the announcement which was also a month before graduation, he made the offer and suggestion that a change would be good for me. I was a little bit offended. It was only a fifteen minute drive on the streets from my house. I would not have to spend thirty to forty-five minutes getting to work among the 405 traffic. I told him that I wanted to think about it.

Later that day, I walked over to the cafeteria and there was a bench of seniors laughing and having a great time. They called me over to let me know they had been remembering a story I had told them about perseverance and not giving up when things got tough when I had tried to fill up a kitty pool for my daughter and I almost gave up because I was running out of time to go pick her up from daycare. I figured out how to fill up the pool with a hollowed out pen and that seeing her smiling face was priceless.

I went to lunch and thought about what the kids shared with me. Later that night, I received an email from a student that was dated from the night before. He thanked me for pushing him to get the best out of him. He thought about me while he was writing a term paper. He said that he appreciated the talk when I told him it's better to have character than be a character.

Chapter Twenty-Two

I thought about the many instances just like that, that I had over the years. But for some reason I went back to those two. I thought to myself, as a teacher, this is as good as it gets. It's not going to be any better here at this school. The next day I went into my principal's office and told him I would take the job at the other school. Athletes talk about wanting to go out on top, especially if they win a championship late in their career. Few athletes get to walk away when they are on top. Most of them hang on too long, and we remember how bad they were at the end of their career. This should have been the moment I went out on top. I should have walked away from teaching. I should have walked away at my peak…but I didn't.

As that thought crossed my mind, one of the staff nurses came in and told me that group is going to start. I turn over and look at the door. I thought about what the doctor suggested for me. I thought about what my roommate said to me about me giving him hope.

I sat up in bed. 'I should go. It's the first day where I was not feeling physically exhausted. Should I go?'

Then I look over at the night stand and I look at my daughter's photo. I need to go, I said. So for the first time in two and half days I got up and went to a group.

We sat in a circle and the therapist asked if anyone would like to share and some people jumped in right away. Some were very honest and insightful, some blamed society, the parents, the police on why they were there in the facility in the first place. They then asked me if I wanted to share. I shared that it was the first time in two days that I finally felt like myself, like I was coming back to normal. But I was struggling to figure out how I got here. I briefly shared my story of the breakdown.

I was a bit worried about leaving, not knowing exactly what sent me into this recent tailspin. I was asked why I needed to know so bad. I paused…*because I want to be a better husband and a better dad when I leave here. I felt by ending up here like I sort of failed them.*

Did your parents fuck you up? *My mother did most of the damage.*
Did you resolve it? *I feel I did.*
Your dad? *Definitely.*
Where were you when the breakdown happened? *I was at work.*
How long have you been a teacher? *This is my 18th year.*
That is what fucked you up! Teaching. All that stress? Who wants all that? You gotta empty your cup. *Empty my cup? What do you mean?*

The fellow patient then shared the story with the groups about emptying your cup…

One particular day, a scholar came to visit the master for advice. "I have come to ask you to teach me about Zen," the scholar said.

Soon, it became obvious that the scholar was full of his own opinions and knowledge. He repeatedly interrupted the master with his own stories and failed to listen to what the master had to say. The master calmly suggested that they should have tea. So the master poured his guest a cup. The cup was filled, yet he kept pouring until the cup overflowed onto the table, onto the floor, and finally onto the scholar's robes.

The scholar cried "Stop! The cup is full already. Can't you see?"

"Exactly," the Zen master replied with a smile. "You are like this cup — so full of ideas that nothing more will fit in. Come back to me with an empty cup."

"Sounds like you've given everything to the kids and this job," he said. "There's nothing left to give other than giving up your sanity or worse giving up your life for it. Is that what you want to do?"

I was struck hard by this statement. I wanted to say no it's not what I want, but my ego and sense of duty caused me to pause and think. I said nothing, and ten minutes later the group ended. I headed back to my room kind of confused.

CHAPTER TWENTY-THREE

I was sitting in my room thinking over and over about the man's Zen story and emptying my cup. Then a staff nurse came in and asked if I wanted to attend today's workout. I decided to go. I actually felt good about wanting to attend. The young woman from group sat next to me. She had shared how she tried to kill herself because her boyfriend cheated on her. I saw the bandages on her wrist. It reminded me of Cookie. How a couple of days before her suicide attempt, she got into a bad fight with her then boyfriend. This was a pretty bad beating. It wasn't enough to land her in the hospital but her face was pretty fucked up. I asked her why she stayed with him. She said because she loved him more than anyone she ever loved, even my dad. Then he just left and it was too much for her. I imagine it was too much for this young woman.

After the workout, I had about an hour before lunch. I headed back to my room. I started to think about Cookie and that young woman. Then I thought about the empty cup. How do I empty my cup? I went to lunch thinking about limits and how limited we are. A human being can only take so much. The man in the group was right. Maybe I have given up everything I can give. Maybe I have nothing left when it comes to my profession.

Then I thought about the young woman and Cookie. I thought that all their love they put into those relationships would hold up but they ended up falling apart. They probably thought that if they gave everything that they could to convince those men not to leave, but in some shape or form it happened, and all they were left with was what is left to love? They looked to themselves if that love was there and I believe it wasn't and that burden became too much to carry. I didn't want to admit it but realized that my profession became a burden after eighteen years. If it didn't become a burden, I would have not landed here. My cup was either full or almost full. Was it a burden that I wanted to continue to bear? It is a question that I thought about for a while until the staff nurse came to tell me lunch was ready.

I received a phone call from my wife. I told her how excited I was that she was picking me up and how excited I was to see my daughter. Then I told her about group and the Zen story.

I told her how I struggled with the question for most of the day about whether I wanted to continue to bear the burden of teaching. But what else was I going to do? I'd have to start over. It wouldn't be easy after 18 years and nearing fifty years old.

I told her I think I know what caused the panic attack and me landing in the hospital. I connected the dots and it was the toll that teaching took on me for the past eighteen years. I didn't realize the emotional and physical toll.

I told her I was sorry that I stayed in teaching too long. She agreed. But I also told her that I didn't regret the reasons that I stayed. I just regretted that I allowed that job to do this to me.

Most of the rest of that night during dinner and in the lounge was pretty uneventful. It was the first time in a long time that my mind was not racing and spinning out of control.

There was a woman who they just brought in, and she was very agitated. But she promised to calm down. She came into the lounge, sat down, and moved some drawings. She didn't realize that someone else had been sitting there drawing.

They got into a minor shoving match and the staff had to separate them, and the agitated woman kept screaming at staff not to touch her. Security was called in and had to restrain her. She was escorted back to her room.

I thought that would trigger me and cause me stress, but I was surprisingly calm. I even smiled a bit after that as I watched TV. Even the guy next to me asked me why I was smiling.

I told him "Because I'm going home tomorrow." I stayed in the lounge until lights out. I went to bed feeling like a kid before Christmas. I knew, though, I had to get some sleep. I looked at

Chapter Twenty-Three

my daughter's photo for a while, then I kissed the photo knowing tomorrow that I would be able to kiss her and hug her in person. I wasn't sure at this point who I would be or how I would be going into tomorrow. I couldn't imagine it because I had been so overwhelmed with how to get out of there the quickest way possible and reliving so many moments from my past life. But honestly, I felt very good about tomorrow. I think I felt that way because that day of the panic attack and what I went through, felt like a distant memory, even if it was for a moment and that thought gave me the peace to fall asleep with a clear mind for the first time in four days.

CHAPTER TWENTY-FOUR

The staff nurse came in my room and asked me asked me if I was ready to go home. I stretched out a bit, and even though I was so jacked up from the adrenaline about going home the night before, I did manage to get a really good night's sleep. Honestly, it has been years since the last time I got a good night's sleep like that. I think in the last three days I had slept more than I have in years. The nurse said I would be released once I have an exit interview with my psychiatrist.

At first, I thought, 'no big deal.' But as I laid in my bed for a while. I thought they were going to let me out first thing. I went to the lounge and looked at the clock and realized I'd been waiting for two hours. I went back to my room and was a bit nervous. I was actually scared that they were going to hold me longer.

The staff nurse said that group was going to start in five minutes. During the group, the man then asked me if I emptied my cup. He asked me how I was feeling since I was going to be released today. I told him I was "very happy. Can't wait to see my family." I then told him that I realized what caused my breakdown, that the breakdown was all the stress from the years of teaching. That he was right about it. I told him what I told my wife, that I had stayed too long. He asked me why I did that. I briefly told him what I experienced with my mother then with my dad. I made a vow why I decided to go to therapy. I wanted to be a good husband and a dad, and that's why I chose to go into therapy. I wanted to be there every step of the way for my daughter, and this was the type of job that afforded me that luxury.

Do you feel you have been there for her? Without a doubt, every step of the way. A staff nurse came in and asked to see me in the hallway.

As I left the man asked me, "Are you going to empty your cup?"

I don't know how I am going to do it, but for my family I'm going to fight like hell to do it.

In the hallway, the nurse tells me that my psychiatrist is ready to see me.

I started my exit interview with a psychiatrist. At the end of it, she gave me the option to sit out the rest of the school year if I wanted. Since it was two weeks before Memorial Day and the end of school was only a month away, she was willing to write an off work note until the end of the school year. I honestly wasn't sure. She wrote it anyway as a back plan if it became too overwhelming to go back after I spent some time at home.

CHAPTER TWENTY-FIVE

After the interview, I met with a different staff nurse than the one that gave me my wake up call, and I grabbed my belongings and paperwork and she escorted me to the lobby. She wished me luck. I told her thank you and sat on one of the couches expecting to see my wife. Though I didn't see her at first, I could smell her perfume. I turned, and there she was. I gave her a big hug, and we both cried before we headed out to the parking lot.

While we drove home, I asked my wife if she remembered my wedding toast. I looked at her and told her she was my Josie. I just held her hand and looked at her. I just kept thinking how lucky that she stuck by me. I thought about our whole relationship together.

It was a rough go at first. I was not aware of it at the time, but I was battling depression. She was very aware of it and recommended that I start therapy.

I know she did get a hard time from some of her closest friends because I was still in school. They felt that I was "riding her coat tails" and that I was dating her for her money. Even though I got accepted into grad school, they just couldn't accept me. Years later, I found out that she lost her friendships with them.

After thinking and reflecting over the past seventeen years together, I became quiet. My wife asked me if I was okay because I was quiet for a while. I told her that I wasn't sure where to go from here. I told her that I had a note to stay out of work for the rest of the year. My wife asked what I wanted to do. I told her I didn't know. My wife suggested that I stay out for the rest of the year and go from there.

I told her maybe she's right, but I didn't know because I felt guilty of how unfair it would be to bail out on my students so close to the end of the school year. She told me that I am entitled to a break, that I had given a lot to my job, and I didn't owe anything to anyone.

I then remembered a former student of mine, Karla. I was in my sixth year teaching and I was starting to experience burnout. I had heard teachers go through it, but I didn't think I would go through it, plus I thought I would have moved on from teaching as well. I don't know how it got out there but she asked me after the graduation ceremony if I was leaving. She had tears in her eyes and asked me not to leave, which was ironic since she was graduating and would not be there herself. I felt guilty as hell knowing that I meant so much to my students. I felt I had no choice but to just stay. I kind of felt like I was at that same crossroads at this point in my career after eighteen years.

We were set to pick up our daughter from school in a couple of hours. I sat on the patio furniture in the backyard. I thought back to one time when my mother got into a fight with my grandmother. Later that night, Cookie went on a bender. The next day, Cookie was crying for most of the day.

Cookie told me that she would get her ass beat by grandma almost every day; especially when Grandma Carmen found out that Cookie was talking to boys from the neighborhood. The next day after her bender, we went to an art store. I found that kind of strange because I didn't see her as the artist type. I never saw her draw anything or talk about any kind of art. She then bought a small bottle of ink

She decided to tattoo my Grandma Carmen's name on her thigh with a basic sewing needle and the ink she bought. I told my wife this story when she came out to the backyard patio to sit with me. I told her how desperate Cookie was, as she was tattooing herself, even more desperate than the time she tried to commit suicide. When she tried to commit suicide, to me she seemed determined more than desperate. And seeing her tattoo my grandma's name that I thought she hated was very confusing to me. I told my wife that that is how I felt in my time in the hospital and that I was scared that that type of desperation could happen to me again. My wife reassured me it wouldn't. I just caressed her face and looked at her thanking God and the universe that she is and in my mind will always be here for me.

Chapter Twenty-Five

We went to pick up our daughter. I asked my wife to drop me off at the Target down the street because I didn't want to take a chance on anyone from work seeing me and asking me how I was doing. My wife said she understood and that she would pick up our daughter and then pick me up from the Target. Upon coming back, our daughter bounded out of the car, saying, "Daddy!" It just melted my heart because it took me back to when she was in elementary school and I would pick her up and she would be so excited and say, "Daddy," in the same way. She was a teenager and would just call me *dad*, but not in this moment, and we hugged and cried together before we got into the car.

Once I got in the car, I kept looking at her, and she told us about her day. It was like the photo I held while in the mental facility came alive out of my hand. It was a magical moment. Then I was reminded of her pooh incident. When in kindergarten, she was given the Winnie the Pooh to be taken care of for the weekend. I remember she waited in anticipation for weeks waiting for her turn. I knew every Friday that she didn't get Pooh because she would look so heartbroken because it wasn't her turn yet.

On the Saturday after she finally got Pooh, we went to one of our favorite breakfast places within walking distance down the street. Once we got there and put in our names for the wait, she kept tossing Pooh higher and higher in the air next to an awning for the business next door. I kept telling her she was too close to be careful so Pooh would not end up on the awning. Well, sure enough, Pooh ended up on the awning.

She kept crying for me to get poor old Pooh down. So, I jogged home and got on the ladder and put it in the back of our SUV. I came back and went up on the awning and got the Pooh bear. Part of having the Pooh was you had to keep a journal and pictures. My wife, of course, took a picture of me getting Pooh down from the awning. I remember the hug our daughter gave me. It felt like the same type of hug in that Target parking lot.

I felt so touched and emotional on my car ride home from picking up our daughter and I took in everything. I took in how green the Vincent Thomas Bridge was. I noticed the cruise ship the *Princess Cruise*, the same ship they used for the famous 1970s TV show "The Love Boat." I saw all the cranes that load the heavy metal containers on the docked freight ships; I always remember how those cranes look like metal giraffes in the distance and up close.

As we were crossing the bridge going into Long Beach, my daughter asked me if I was coming back to work. She told me what she went through while I was gone. A lot of rumors were going on around me. I could tell by the strain on her face as she told me what was going on and how it weighed on her. One student in particular spread a rumor that I didn't take enough medication and that is why I was not a school. "I guess he didn't take his Adderall," he joked and unfortunately my daughter overheard this. She wanted to punch him in the face she told me.

She told me that she didn't want me to go back to work because she didn't want to see me go through that again. I was honest with her and told her that it was something that I needed to think about. I could tell she was disappointed to hear that, so I changed the subject and asked her how our dog, Lucy, was doing and if she was taking good care of her while I was gone. She nodded and managed to smile a bit.

After we had dinner, I went out onto our patio in the backyard. I just loved the peace and quiet of our backyard. My wife had a vision of what she wanted the backyard to look like and how especially she wanted the lighting to be. It turned out really great, and when I needed a break from the world I found myself back here a lot. My wife joined me and asked me what I am thinking about. I told her about the scene in the movie, "The Shawshank Redemption" and how Andy tells Red that hope was a good thing. I told my wife that self-sacrifice is not always a good thing. That that is what most likely landed me in the hospital

I told her my head is telling me I shouldn't go back, but my heart is telling me to go back because of a sense of duty. My dad always told me to finish what you start, and I wanted to finish the school year because of that sense of duty I had within me. I feel like it is in my DNA.

But I felt more confused than ever. My wife told me she was going to go back in the house. She then looked at me one more time and told me that she knew I would make the right decision. I told her I just didn't know what the right decision was, and I wanted to know now at this moment. She then said, "God always gives us the answers, but it is always in His time, not ours. You'll figure it out." I just kept staring at the lights and the landscaping, looking for some type of sign or answer.

A little while after, my dad called to see how I am doing. I told him some of the details about my stay in the hospital. I told him that

Chapter Twenty-Five

I think that I have stayed in teaching too long, that the years of stress just took a toll on me that I could not at that point handle. He then asked me if I am going back to work. I told him I am not sure. At the end of the conversation, he told me that it may be in my best interest to just stay away for a while, at least until the school year ends, and just focus on whether you want to go back next year.

As I drove to get some stuff from the store, I listened to the song, *Blue in Green*, by Miles Davis. The tone and melody told me it's a song about someone special who stands by your side, especially during a difficult time. I teared up because I thought about my wife. I imagined in the song, the guy is having a rough go and sitting on the bed just feeling down and trying to figure things out. He saw his girlfriend or wife come in and does not say a word once she sees the look on his face. She just sits and puts her hand on his back and just rubs his back as if to say, 'everything will be fine.' I remembered thinking that I had always hoped to someday find a woman like that. One that just knows and doesn't have to say a word. Who doesn't feel the need to fix things but to just be with her man.

I remembered when I was dating my wife before we were married, after about six months, I could feel that I was falling for her. I didn't want to say anything. When it came to love, I always felt like I was a jinxed man. I've always had the courage to tell a girl or woman how I felt, but it seemed like I would always crash and burn. I decided to talk about it with my roommate all the time. I worried about whether she was felt the same way or if she didn't at all. I worried about asking her that question and her saying no. He paused and told me that you already know. I'm wasn't afraid she was going to say no. I was more worried about her saying yes.

That just felt like I took a good football hit. He was so right. I thought about it for a couple of days, then she invited me to her condo. We had finished a beer together, and I just decided to let it fly. I told her how I felt, and she told me she felt the same way. I then kissed her and just held her hand, like the way the guy in the song *Blue in Green* would have.

For the next several months, things were great. We got up late on a Saturday. She met with her real estate agent, as she was looking to buy a house. She came back and started talking but kept pausing, then kept repeating, "I'm ok, I'm ok," and she rushed into the shower.

I couldn't make heads or tails of it. I was confused because she already took a shower before she left. Then I heard a loud *thud* in the bathroom. I rushed into the bathroom and she was on the bathtub floor convulsing. I called 911, and they rushed her to the hospital.

Later on, the doctor told me she was conscious and alert and that I could go in the room. He told me she had suffered a seizure. We later found out she had congenitalAVM, which meant she had been born with brain vessels that were tangled in a knot, and it could disrupt normal blood flow in the brain. I went in and just held her hand for a while. While I was in the lobby of the hospital waiting to see her, I talked to my stepmom on the phone and told her what happened. My stepmom told me you need to tell her how you feel.

I looked at my girlfriend and simply said, "I'm sorry this had to happen for me to tell you I love you." We then hugged and she cried in my arms.

As I kept driving to the store, then toward the end of the song, I thought about how she had always been there by my side every step of the way, even when I was in the hospital, I felt she was with me. I then thought about, do I want to put her through this again? I know that is such a stupid thought because of the chances of it happening again were slim, but it still crossed my mind and I just did not want her to suffer something like this again.

A couple of weeks later, things seemed to be getting back to normal and we decided on going on a weekend getaway. It was not really a getaway but more like a staycation because we stayed local in Venice, which is only 30-45 minutes away. I then got a phone call from a former colleague and friend telling me Dwan Hurt had passed away. He was the dean at the first school I worked at, and we became really close. We were good at pranking each other.

To know that he just passed was so shocking. My buddy told me his funeral was the next day. So, I went home real quick and grabbed a suit and headed back to the staycation hotel we were staying at and the next day I attended the funeral. I was still in shock because he was so young. At the time he was in his fifties.

Once the service was over, I was swarmed by a bunch of former students. It was so awesome to see how they were doing. A lot of them were professionals, some were doctors and lawyers and directors of companies. It was pretty awesome. We all swapped some old stories.

We sat around for about an hour and a half before everyone headed to the reception. They asked me if I was still teaching. I told them yes but I was on break because of my health. The students were telling me how I was their favorite teacher of all time. It meant a lot to hear that, but I was very confused about where, professionally and somewhat personally, to go from here.

When I got back to the hotel after the funeral, I talked to my wife about the services and the eulogy and what they said about Dwan, and teachers I saw that she knew and some of the stories I shared with the students.

I told her that even though officially it was heart failure, it was the job that killed him. He gave too much to that job. She asked me if I want to end up like that? I told her no.

The Monday after we got back from our little staycation, I got an email from a former student who graduated two years prior. What first struck me about the email was the time stamp. It was 2:30 am. He was thanking me for always pushing him to do better. When I first taught him, he was a challenge. He was your typical class clown, which I could handle, but the challenge came in when he was held accountable for when he was crossing over the line. He had a hard time accepting responsibility for his actions, especially when it negatively impacted the class.

I finally pulled him aside and told him, "I know you probably get a kick out of the other kids laughing and you get some type of charge out of it. But what you don't see is that many times they are laughing at you, not with you. You have to decide whether you want to be a character or have character."

He reminisced in the email about that story and how much it meant to him once he started to attend college. He sent it at that time because he was working on an essay, and it reminded him about the times in my class, especially when I had to discipline him. He learned that in life you have to discipline yourself in order to achieve what you are attempting to achieve. He was learning this concept in that moment in the middle of the night, and that meant a lot to me that he took time out to reach out to me.

CHAPTER TWENTY-SIX

As a result of that email, I thought about my current students. It got me seriously thinking about going back, but then I thought about the day I had my breakdown and ultimately decided I was still not ready to go back. It was probably best that I stay out for the remainder of the school year.

About a week after receiving that email, I looked up at the calendar. I noticed that there were three weeks left in the school year. Later that day, my daughter came home from school. She shared with me that a lot of my students were complaining because they did not feel like they were going to do well on the final. I started to think about that email again and kept thinking about how I impacted his life and many students' lives over the years, especially after Dwan's funeral how grown up they had become in the way they spoke, the professional positions they held, the cars they drove, the way they dressed. I was so impressed by them, and yet they thanked me and the other teachers that were there at the funeral service.

Out of nowhere, I asked my daughter how she would feel if I came back to work the rest of the year? I asked her if she felt the same frustration as the other students about the upcoming final. She said yeah, but she didn't want me to come back just because she was frustrated. She then asked me if I had asked mom the same question. No, but I plan to talk to her about it.

We sat on the sofa, and I told her what was going on in my mind in regards to possibly going back. I then retold her about the time I decided to leave my first teaching gig but how I wanted one more year to prove myself and how I saw the writing on the wall and they didn't really want me to come back for another year.

She shared her concerns with me and did not pressure me either way. She was very pragmatic about the situation, which I did not expect at all. I thought she would be definitely talking me off the ledge sort of speak. To her credit, she then told me that if that is how I felt I should go back but that she still is very concerned about the stress of going back would involve and if I was prepared for that. I nodded my head saying I could handle it.

The next day, I called my principal and told her that I would return on Monday. My principal kept asking me if I was sure. Actually, I was not sure. But I would my best to make sure I finished the year with those kids.

As I pulled in the parking lot, funny, awkward thoughts and emotions were going through me. I remembered a scene from the movie, *Pushing Tin*, with John Cusack, Billy Bob Thorton, and Angelina Jolie. It was about the day in the lives of air traffic controllers. One controller had a nervous breakdown. For months he would try to go back to work. He would see the other traffic controllers at the door ready to greet him and he would just turn around and race to his car and rush home. This time around, he got all the way to the front door. All the traffic controllers were behind the lobby doors watching him get out of his car. As he was getting out of his car, they started to take odds on how far he would make it. He got up all the way up to the front doors where they all greeted and welcomed him to come into the building. He took one step forward and suddenly he raced back to his car and rushed home again. I think the characters that were played by John Cusack and Billy Bob Thorton joked that's the furthest he's ever been.

We teachers had similar bets on new teachers that were hired, and we would take odds on the teacher that was most likely to leave before the end of the school year. I remember one new teacher who came along in my fifth year of teaching. We had a high turnover from the year before, and I think we hired like five new teachers. There was this nun, Sister Sharon. She was probably in her mid to late sixties, and she just out of the blue felt like she wanted to teach.

That year, I had my first period off, so I had gone to the copier room to make extra copies. There was Sister Sharon, flustered,

red-faced, and sweaty trying to figure out how to make copies. I went over to help her. The copier was jammed, and she had no idea how to fix it. It's understandable. Honestly, it looked like it had been a while since she made her way around a copier machine. So I cleared out the jams for her. I asked her if this was her prep period as well, and she said no that her class was waiting on her for the copies. I asked her if there was anyone watching her class. She looked shocked and said, "Do we need to have someone watch our class?" I told her yes because of liability issues.

Later that day, the odds of who was going to leave first came up, and based on what I had seen with Sister Sharon struggling with the copier, her age, and her total lack of experience, she had too much against her to last the semester. I, at least in my head, thought she would be lucky to last the week based on the 'deer in headlights' look she had on her face. You could tell in that moment in the copier room she was way in over her head. I was going to chime in, but I couldn't do it. First of all, she was a nun, and I did not want to gamble my chances between heaven and hell, and I was not cold enough to express those kinds of sentiments.

But after the bell rang, I leaned over to my buddy J.D. and said, "If I were a betting man, Sister Sharon won't last a week."

Sure enough, she was gone midweek. In a weird way, I wondered if those same odds were being bet against me. Frankly, I was just me putting pressure on myself.

CHAPTER TWENTY-SEVEN

So, the following Monday, after about two weeks, I showed up to class and suddenly got nervous. My blood pressure went up a tad. Not to the level that I felt the day I had my breakdown, but just a twinge of rising blood pressure which took me back to that moment in the classroom when I rushed out and headed down the street to the paramedics.

More and more kids started to pour into the classroom, and I got more and more nervous. I started to question whether this was the right decision. Part of me wanted to run, but part of me wanted to get it together and finish strong. I wanted to be able to say to myself that I was able to push through this stressful and adverse filled moment.

As I was in the doorway nervously greeting the students entering the class, I happen to see my daughter walking down the hall to her class. She saw me waiting by the door for the students to enter the class. She had the same smile that she had in the picture I had with me in the mental facility.

She mouthed to me, "Have a good day, Dad."

I smile back at her, and in my head I decided 'Yes, I'm going to have a good day.'

The tardy bell rangs, and I enter the classroom ready to go.

I wish I could report any difficulties and drama from that point, but everything went smoothly, and we all made it through finals in one piece. A lot of the kids showed their gratitude and thanked me for coming back to finish the year with them and said they looked forward to seeing me around next year.

At graduation that year, besides honoring the students and naming the valedictorian and salutatorian, they would name the teacher of the year. Before the students are honored, they announce the teacher of the year award. It was me. Honestly, I was in complete shock. And then I teared up, as I shook the principal's hand. It was so meaningful to me because I know that the students vote on this award.

As I walked up to the stage, the kids went nuts. After receiving my award, I headed back to my seat and heard several kids yell out, "We love you, Rivera!"

I told them "I love you too!"

I looked at my award and realize how much I've given to my career, but I wondered if it is enough love to bring me back next year? I fluctuated between *maybe* and *no*, but *yes* never entered my mind. I looked up at the kids and the administration.

The administration began to honor the kids and I thought to myself, 'We will just have to wait and see.'

CHAPTER TWENTY-EIGHT

A couple weeks after graduation, I opened my email and saw that my current principal sent a list of days and times to come in and sign our contracts for the next year. Days before, I heard rumors that our Athletic Director was leaving to pursue another career. I never really wanted to move into an admin position, but I always told myself and my wife that the Altletic Director was definitely a position that interested me.

Once I got my time and day to sign my returning contract, I went home and talked to my wife. My biggest worry was going back into the classroom. If it were up to me at that moment, I would not have gone back into teaching based on what happened weeks prior, and even though the rest of the weeks I had remaining before finals and into finals went smoothly and without incident, I was having serious doubts about going back into the classroom. I felt stuck.

If I left, I would have to start all over, and that was not ideal. I was approaching fifty. I would have to start a new career with no experience other than being a teacher and my daughter just finished her first year of high school and played club volleyball. I know I could not afford to leave, and even if I found another job outside of teaching, I had a gut feeling it was not going to pay me as much as I was making, even though as a Catholic School teacher we got paid a lot less than public school teachers. I knew at that point, the best card

I had to play was to gamble on whether the rumor that the Athletic Director was leaving was true. That was my best bet. The only issue was that as the AD, you would still have to teach three classes. I didn't like that part, but it was better than teaching five classes. So there was a bit of a tradeoff. My wife fully supported me and thought it was a good gamble, but we understood the downside, that I would have to return to the stressful environment of teaching. I did have some leverage because I was a very successful coach at the school and since I worked there, I saw firsthand what the job duties and responsibilities entailed.

It did interest me and I would have to teach, but it would not be, at least in my head, my sole focus. That's what I loved about coaching. It gave me focus and distracted me from the day-to-day stress of teaching.

So when it was my turn for my contract signing appointment, I expressed to my principal that I am very interested in the AD position. As soon as I said that, she had a small smile on her face and said I would be a perfect fit for the position and I was offered the job and even more relieved to know that I would not have to teach any classes. That was a huge relief, and when I got home and told my wife, she hugged me and was excited and happy and relieved for me as well.

So, a week after school was out and transitioning into summer school and the sports programs, I started the new job. I already knew I had my hands full when I saw the condition of the AD office. It was a mess, and I knew it was going to take days to clean it. I spent probably three days cleaning out the office. We also had a cargo bin situated behind the weight room. I opened it and I had my work cut out for me. There were uniforms strewn everywhere and a lot of old uniforms that were outdated and not being used. Little did I know this would be an omen how stressful this job was going to be.

But my primary job was to make sure that the athletes that were participating in the summer programs were up to date with their physicals and their athletic clearance information on the school website under the athletics page. After a couple of months, the AD job wasn't what I thought it was going to be.

Football season was even worse. There were so many moving parts. It was very difficult at the time because we played our football games off-campus, and it's not like there was some checklist or handbook to know what to do. I got the avalanche of information as it came in. I had to reserve parking spots for the referees and our team trainer. Most of the time, people would move the cones and

Chapter Twenty-Eight

take the spots which just caused more chaos. I had to call a bunch of volunteers – one for the scoreboard, a couple for announcing the games, other volunteers to set up the PA system. After about the first three or four games, I hated football and hated even watching a football game on TV.

I still was a little optimistic because I was able to go to all of my daughter's volleyball games. I was there physically but not very present at all. I had so much crammed in my head over this job. I honestly thought, as far as the stress, that it would not be that bad being the AD because I did not have to teach any classes, I could watch all the sports I want, and I could come in at 11am since I had to stay late for football games and later basketball and soccer games.

But I didn't realize how much I was in over my head, until my wife noticed. She said she was watching me supervise my daughter's volleyball game, and that I looked like a shell of myself. My eyes looked glazed over, and I did not talk much for the rest of the school year. My boss even started to notice how overwhelmed I looked at each weekly administrative meeting we had.

Then, right around after Thanksgiving, my boss called me and told me she empathized with how I was overwhelmed with this job. She told me that I can transition into another position. It was ironic because, after talking to my wife, I was planning to have a meeting with her, as I did not want to continue being the AD. It was like she had read my mind. She told me the following week I would switch with the current librarian, and he would be the AD until they recruited a new one next year, and I would be the librarian. I can't begin to tell you how relieved I was to hear that.

What was also great was I would get an additional stipend for opening the library an hour before school. For my nerves and my emotional state, this was great. No stress at all and not a lot of responsibility except cataloging books and monitoring and assisting students before school, break, and after school.

From January until the end of the school year, it was great not having the day-to-day stress of being a teacher. For some reason, I thought I could get used to this for the long haul. This would be great if I could be in this position until the end of my career.

Going into my second year, for the most part it was looking like that would be the case, especially when March came around even though we were about to live in a world of uncertainty when the coronavirus pandemic hit us. Justifiably so, it sent our world in a panic, and many were scrambling to find out what to do next. After months of isolation and wearing masks, and testing and sanitizing, there was social distancing and for the teachers and students, distance learning through Zoom.

Even though, for day-to-day operations of the school for teachers and students were shut down, we kept the library open for students who needed computers or extra help to complete their school work. So I spent the rest of that year just keeping the library open. At the end of the year, though, our Dean of Curriculum came in and asked me if I wanted to go back to teaching, and I told him I was fine being in the library.

So I was in the library for one more year and we made it through COVID. Things seem to be chugging along until the end of the 2021-22 school year. In June, when I went in to sign my contract. I didn't think anything of it, then my boss told me that this would be the last year that I would be able to work in the library. She told me that she could not justify in a budget for me being a librarian and receiving a teacher's salary. So, I signed my contract to be the librarian for one more year. I was numb. All I kept thinking was, 'Oh shit, I gotta go back to the classroom.' When I got home I talked to my wife about it and at that moment, rationally understood that my boss could no longer have me in the library. I got it, but for some reason it still felt a bit like a kick in the stomach.

Then, a month later, somewhere probably around the second or third week in July, my cousin Marcos from New Jersey called me and said the following week he was coming on his annual visit to California to visit his daughter who lived in San Diego. That following week, the early morning before he was set to meet us in L.A. for dinner, I got up suddenly, and it scared the shit out of me how I felt. My anxiety was as high as it was the morning I had my manic episode that landed me in the mental health facility.

I put on my workout clothes, rushed to the gym, and worked for about 45 minutes. My anxiety subsided but was still a little bit there after my workout, so I hit the cardio machines for about another 45 minutes. Then, I decided, after my workout, to go take a long walk on the beach. The sun had just risen, and I walked until the sky was sunny and clear blue. I called my wife and told her what happened and asked me if we should cancel getting together with my cousin Marcos. I told her no and that I was feeling better, and I didn't really want him to know this and what happened to me three years ago. So, I got home, we got ready, and met my cousin and I made it through the rest of the day and evening without incident.

Chapter Twenty-Eight

I just don't really know what the hell happened to me. After a couple of weeks, I talked about what could possibly happen with my wife. I was totally unsure at that time in July, but things seemed to crystalize for me. I think it was connected to the fact that I knew after the upcoming school year that I would have to go back to the classroom. After a long talk with my wife, I told her I'm not sure if I want to or ready to go back into the classroom. She asked me what I was going to do. I told I wasn't sure. That I just have to play this year out and in the meantime get my resume out there and look at other jobs that are not teacher or even education related, other than maybe admissions or counseling at the college level. But, I will just have to see what comes my way until the following June.

CHAPTER TWENTY-NINE

It was weird, for two years I felt no anxiety, no fear, no worry. Then once I was told I was going back into the classroom, I felt edgy or scared most days. I'd over worry and over think, but I seemed okay. I was just flat terrified about going back to the classroom. The nice thing about being in the library is I didn't have to deal with being in the classroom, dealing with students, dealing with parents or the day to day stressors that seemed to have landed me in the hospital in the first place.

Then, after about a month into the school year, I headed to the bathroom. It was hot day, typical of August weather, so all the classroom doors were propped open. As I walked, I could hear the collective voices of teachers lecturing and of students talking about what happened the past weekend.

Out of nowhere, I had this tingling feeling start to overcome my fingers then I hit what I call the "oh no zone." It's similar shot in a horror movie or a scene of intense drama, and the camera zooms on the characters face at 100 miles per hour with intense suspenseful music playing. Then, that tingling feeling in your finger overtakes your body. Every time I've had a panic attack, it started that way.

I rushed to the bathroom as quick as I could. I took a pee so it would distract me from focusing on the tingling feeling before it turned into absolute terror. I washed my hands and splashed water on my face to see if I would feel better, but it didn't work. I pulled my phone out of my pocket and called my wife. She was able to calm me down and suggested I make an appointment with a therapist and my psychiatrist.

On the way home that afternoon, I got lucky and was able to get an appointment with a therapist and my psychiatrist. I had talked to both and told them what happened. My psychiatrist gave me an additional medication to my mood stabilizing medicine that was for anxiety.

For a couple of days, I was ok, but then I walked by the classrooms and again I was triggered halfway to the bathroom. I got to the bathroom and was so petrified I could not pee. The anxiety flared pretty bad. For some reason, I turned and looked at the door. I put my hands on the door and rested my forehead on the door and fucked up thoughts were swirling around my head:

'Am I going to commit suicide over this?'

'Are we going to go bankrupt and lose everything?'

'Am I going to have to find a new job since I cannot work in the library anymore?'

Then my worst fears came up:

'Am I going to end in another 72-hour hold in the mental hospital?'

'Am I going to be held indefinitely?

Am I going to have to be in for the rest of my life wearing a straightjacket?'

I took some deep breaths, then I started to do an exercise I learned online when you are having panic attacks called panoramic breathing. It's a technique where you first look in front of you in the distance. You take deep breaths, then without moving you head, only your eyes you let them travel in a panoramic fashion while focusing on your breathing. So, I walked out of the restroom, walked out to the breezeway where I could see the Vincent Thomas Bridge in the distance. I started the exercise and about 15 minutes I felt better, and I knew it was fifteen minutes later because I looked at my phone.

I headed back to the library and my buddy and coworker in the library, Greg, looked at me and said, "Did you take a dump?"

"Yeah," I said. "We ate Mexican last night. I had a wet burrito."

When Greg focused back on the screen work on the school newsletter, I grabbed my medication out of my lunch bag and snuck my anxiety pill out and took the pill so he wouldn't notice. I started back on what I was doing on the computer and a little while later, I could not tell you how much time elapsed, the medication kicked in

Chapter Twenty-Nine

and helped me remain calm for a while. The bottle said, take one a day as needed, and from there on out, if I needed the medication, I would just take it, even though I could not stand medication. It just reminded me of all the drug use I witnessed as a kid.

As a result of all this, I stopped using the bathroom upstairs, and I walked down the stairs just to use the bathroom. I also avoided using the bathroom during school breaks and school wide lunch at all costs.

Other than having to figure what route I was going to take to the bathroom, everything was sailing around smoothly. That was until Labor Day weekend. My parents live near the water in Redondo Beach, and when it comes to long weekends, we usually stay at their house as a staycation because they typically go out of town during that time. My wife and daughter like to spend time in the pool, but I like the fact I do not have to pay for a hotel and there are good restaurants within walking distance.

For some reason, I told them I did not want to go the first night. I guess I was feeling sorry for my dog and leaving her by herself; I felt guilty even though in the past we would go away for the weekend she would be fine. So, I just ate, kicked back, and watched Netflix.

I was feeling a little tired so I headed off to bed ready to go to sleep. I then started to feel real edgy. Then, I thought about what if my wife is not with me by the end of our lives? Am I going to go into a full blown panic? I kept thinking I don't want to lose my wife, and the anxiety got worse. I raced to the backyard, stood on my deck, and did the panoramic breathing. Panoramic Breathing. Then, I took my medication simultaneously. After about twenty minutes, I started to get centered. I called my wife and told her that I changed my mind that I was coming over to join them. I got there and before we went to bed I told her what happened and I just sat at the edge of the bed and teared up and cried lightly.

"Am I going to go through this forever?"

"No," wife said, as she rested her hand on my shoulder

"I wish I was as confident as you and my psychiatrist."

"You'll be able to raise your confidence. Give it time," she said.

"Yeah, but you know what my biggest fear is?"

"What's that?"

"That I won't be able to see you anymore. I'm scared if you pass away what am I going to do? I think I would go crazy."

"No you won't. We will be together at the end of our lives. Just like the movie *The Notebook*," she said with a smile.

I then smiled too but was still terrified as hell at the prospect of her not being around. "And also my biggest fear, that I am going to end up back at the mental facility and won't ever be able to come home."

"That's your mind screwing with you," she said.

"Maybe you're right," I said. "My psychiatrist feels similar. I asked him if I will ever end up back in the mental facility. He said no, but at this point in my life, I'm not totally convinced."

"We would not say it if we did not believe it," she said. "It's just a matter of you believing it."

"Yeah, I guess you're right. I just wonder when that is going to happen."

"In its own time, not ours. Why don't we try to go to sleep." We talked for a bit longer then fell asleep and despite what happened I had a good sleep that night.

CHAPTER THIRTY

That episode happened in September. For the most part, from then until February, things again were smooth. Then, on February 2, I was on my way to work I listened to the song, *Thinking of You* by Lenny Kravitz. I don't know why, but I just wanted to listen to it. I played it twice and both times I teared up. I mostly teared up at the lyrics.

It's a song of remembrance, a tribute of tenderness for his mother who had passed away. I thought of Cookie. I thought maybe I was tearing up because I was feeling that same tenderness, but when I thought about it more, it was more this profound sadness. Sadness because I wish that Cookie was tender and loving like that I could feel those same feelings and sentiments that Lenny did when he wrote that song. I'm sad that I am still affected by the way that Cookie treated me. I'm not bitter about it anymore; I'm just sad. And what's sad is my stepmom didn't treat me like that and I do consider her my mom, but since it was not Cookie, it's not the same, and that is why the sadness is deeply ingrained in me, even though I wish it weren't. I still feel like a part of me has been cut off. I guess I didn't realize it still hurts.

The next morning, I again listened to *Thinking of You* while going to work. I took a big risk and listened to it while our daughter was in the car. I really teared up, and wondered, 'Why I am tearing up?' I guessed because in the song he wants his mom to be proud of him, and I think he realized from up above his mom was proud of him because he was able to write this beautiful song. He was all the things that his mom wanted him to be. I got really sad thinking about that. I wished Cookie wanted that for me. Maybe she did but couldn't because of her own demons. I wish I had it in me to miss Cookie in that way but it's not in me. Maybe my sadness is a way of missing her. Cookie and I could've had that type of relationship and I am deeply saddened that we didn't.

Then I realized yesterday was her birthday. Maybe she's trying to talk to me. Just sad.

Later that day when I got home, I talked about the last two days with my wife about those two experiences involving Cookie.

"I believe she is trying to contact you," she said.

"Maybe you are right," I said.

"I know you may not agree, but she was a great lady."

"Why do you say that?"

"Because she had you, and you are the man of my dreams."

I teared up when she said that and she gave me a big old hug.

"Moms are always a part of us," she said. "I am forever grateful to Cookie because you are my person."

We then changed and took our dog for a walk.

CHAPTER THIRTY-ONE

After Cookie's birthday, I started to research a lot about anxiety and panic attacks. I discovered this guy on YouTube called The Anxiety Guy. He knew exactly the kinds of things I was going through with my anxiety. I started to follow him, and then I found out he had his own web page and you can take seminars, and he had all these resources. But I kept it simple and just watched his video to the point I subscribed to his channel. Then I came across a video of daily anxiety affirmations. I started to listen to them while on my to work each day. It was about a 30-minute video, so it was perfect amount of time while I drove to work, and sometimes I would listen on the way home. One affirmation was I am bigger than my thoughts and emotions. That, especially if I was struggling with anxiety, helped me get centered.

Then, in all my research I stumbled across a book called, *Rewire Your Anxious Brain: How to use the Neuroscience of Fear to end Anxiety, Panic, and Worry.* This book was a game changer for me. It probably is the best nonfiction book I have ever read. If you struggle with any type of anxiety, this is a must read. It gives you background on anxiety and how it works in the brain and gives you practical exercises in how to cope with anxiety.

My greatest take away is how anxiety works two ways. First, in the cortex of your brain conscious thoughts trigger your anxiety, and second in your amygdala. Discussion about the amygdala blew my mind. The author's talk about how the amygdala is our fight or flight response in the brain, and as part of our evolution that response reacts to fear and danger, but what caught my attention was that the amygdala has memories of its own that are triggered by fear but because they are not in your cortex it can fire up for what you think at first is nothing at all.

A great example that was used in the book was a Vietnam veteran who was having constant panic attacks in the bathroom. Over time, with the help of his therapist, they figured out why his amygdala was firing up every time he set foot in the shower. He noticed that his wife had switched soaps. He then realized it was the same soap he used while he was in Vietnam. Man, it was fascinating and it made sense of my responses to fear.

For a long time, I was not afraid of anything. It got to the point that could not remember the last time I was fearful from my days with Cookie. I mostly could tell you I dealt with a lot of sadness and anger, but fear, looking back on my therapy, that part of my mental difficulties was something that simply did not come up. I think all the years of suppressing my fear came to the surface and helped fan the flames of fear that landed me in the mental facility and what I am going through now.

Once I did the exercises of the anxiety guy, the affirmations, and reading this book, it seemed day by day I was getting better and better. But there were still days I struggled. I think at this point what I was struggling with was handling stress the best I have ever dealt with, even in the days I was in therapy working on my depression. I felt really good and blessed, and now I realize when I feel that way, subconsciously I want to hold on to that as long as I can. I don't want to let go and be organic and that is what I think is causing part of the anxiety that I'm still getting used to being organic instead of being so regimented. I am so proud of myself that I am taking my internal work and taking it to a new level. I've done it mostly on my own as far as getting help and getting educated on my disability. The anxiety guy says you have to look at creating positive outcomes of coping and eventually eliminating anxiety instead of prevention. That seems to me more of an attainable goal for my subconscious rather than prevention.

However, there was a drawback. After I had that near panic attack on Labor Day weekend, my psychiatrist told me to take two pills a day as needed. The medication worked very well for me on top of my fitness and training regimen. I was having some side effects though.

Chapter Thirty-One

I would get headaches sometimes and would be bloated and gassy. I told my library buddy Greg about it and he told me about a cousin of his that struggles with anxiety, and he said that his cousin was taking CBD oil. I did some research on it and was looking into edibles as well because I did not want to smoke weed in particular. I like the feeling of getting high on weed, but did not like that I had to smoke to get there, and so that made edibles really appealing to me.

I then emailed my psychiatrist to see what he had to say about it. Later that morning, around 11:30am, I got a response. At first it seemed a positive email. He said it would not hurt to try it, but he warned me to only take CBD oil that does not have THC in it. THC is not good for people with bipolar disorder.

When I read that I said, "What the hell?" Then I wrote him a follow up email that I was confused because when I was leaving the mental facility, my wife and I were told that it was a general anxiety disorder. He emailed me back and said that I had a manic episode and that is why I have bipolar disorder. I was shocked at first.

I just emailed my wife that am proud of the good things I've done for myself lately. So this is a bit of a blow to absorb right now. But I just gotta keep doing the work I am doing and just take it one step at a time. Continue with my affirmations and workout, eat right, relieve my stress, see the positive, embrace mistakes.

Despite reading what I just read, I felt calm and not panicked and not letting my mind race. I'm just sad for some reason. Maybe I am feeling deep empathy for Cookie. I think maybe subconsciously I'm feeling for her struggles because she did not have the long term resources to help her out. That is why she died prematurely. But I'm concerned because maybe my daughter has it, and that kind of scares me. *These are 'what ifs?'* And in my experience with my struggles, what ifs are what caused my mind and heart to race and spin out of control.

This is what is currently going through my mind: One step at a time, One day at a time one action at a time. It will take time to break my unconscious mind pattern to delve into negativity and relive past traumas.

Let's face it, my willingness to go to therapy for my depression opened the door for me to go through all this healing process. I was able to get a Bachelor's and Master's and marry the woman of my dreams and have the greatest daughter in the world. I'm embracing my life the best I can and trying to live it to the fullest. That's all I can ask of myself. Especially going through what I am going through. Things can be a lot worse. With God's grace and family support I will do well through this. God knows that I can handle this. And he is giving the power to do that. I've not only been here for myself but for my daughter. God is showing me that I am strong because I've managed to live a fulfilled life so far, even though at times I have felt unfulfilled. I realize now that God has been telling me that I already have a life worth living and that I don't need that external love from the world like being the greatest athlete and being the greatest writer. I am great, especially as a dad and a husband and I'm getting better every day and I don't need to dwell on my worry. This is an opportunity to be an example to my daughter. To teach her that worry does us no good. That we have to enjoy the life we have and not think that external things are going to give us that joy. Simple, beautiful things are the key. This is a reminder how much God loves us and has faith in us. The good thing is, even though this is difficult what I had to go through, that God has been here the whole time. It's just these things I had to go through maybe to test my faith. Not for God but for myself. It is truly a miracle that I am at this point in my life. All this after I emailed my wife and told her what the psychiatrist said and she said that label does define who you are. I was pretty calm before, but when she said that to me it took this huge weight off my shoulders and took away the temporary shock I was experiencing and that is why I had thoughts of clarity even though I found out a hard truth about myself.

It seemed the only mountain to climb that was left was to meet with my principal about my status for next year. I was really nervous. I did not know what was going to happen. My anxiety started to focus on the possibility of not having a job the next year. I felt that possibility was real. So I emailed my principal to set up a meeting and she agreed that would be great that we could meet next Thursday after lunchtime.

I was headed to my meeting with my principal and felt a sense of calm. I told her about my concerns, most importantly was - would I even have a job next year? She assured me I would and she would never let me go because I was very valuable to the campus. She knew how much the community appreciated me for being here. The only couple of things that did not go well was I was not going to be able to teach PE. I most likely would be back to English, possibly teaching seniors, which kind of sucked because I would have to teach AP English, but I guess beggars can't be choosers. But she was going to ask if the freshman teacher could move up and teach seniors so I could go back to the Freshman. So, I prayed for that scenario to happen. And I committed to summer school. I needed to brush up and get my stuff prepared for the summer. But I didn't need to do it right that second.

I felt a little nervous after the meeting. I think it was because mainly I'll be rusty coming back in the classroom.

I could feel myself clenching a bit, but it would be fine. I just needed to work through these symptoms and go from there. Overall, I had to believe that it was going to be different in the classroom this time around. I knew I could not have a savior complex or a perfectionist attitude. I just had do my best to not compromise my mental health and well-being. I just needed to do my best and not feel I have to be the best. And once that day was done, I will get the hell out of there and stick to my wellness routines, get in some golf and plan fun weekends. I need to plan more to meet with friends and do something to decompress from the week instead of what I was doing and sleep in for most of Saturday and lesson planning Sunday's.

I'm not sure how to articulate this thought, but I need to do the bare minimum to keep my job and benefits. I can't throw my heart and soul into this. I can't look to coach a sport or moderate or anything like that. I just needed to make my wellness and taking care of my family the priority, rather than trying to have all the students in an AP class pass the AP test. I can't have a perfectionist attitude.

Another factor was I think I was scared and anxious and I realized I would be back in the classroom. I had not stepped in a classroom or interacted as a teacher with students in three years. Plus, I was scared because I am not as prepared as I would like to be. That was my control issues kicking in. I knew that. I just had to do the best I could. I could dwell on the frustration of being told earlier what I would be teaching and the fear of being fearful of what happened in the classroom three years ago. I needed to constantly affirm myself that I am not my thoughts. I am not the person I was three years ago. I have to embrace that or I am going to let my fears take over and I actually have control over that.

CHAPTER THIRTY-TWO

Started Summer School classes yesterday. I thought I would be a lot more nervous than I was. I felt very comfortable. Like I never left, but the difference was that I was more Zen, I was more centered. I took my time. I didn't jump around the lesson in order to get the class over and done with. I scaffolded nicely. I built on a concept one on top of the other. I did feel a bit of tension this morning but felt better once I did my meditations, affirmations and muscle relaxation exercises. It helped that I only have to teach two classes with a maximum of eight students in each of the classes.

Toward the end of summer school, I ran into my colleague, Lauren Adams. I just spent an hour talking to her. I shared with her how I came full circle back to teaching. I told her my experience of what happened to me three years ago. I was so touched and supported after I told her my story – all the trauma, the setbacks and the triumphs. At the end of the conversation, she gave me a big hug and said she was proud of me and happy to have me back in the English Department.

It was finally the last day of summer school. I felt excited and ready to wrap up, even though technically I have one more day, but it is a day without students unless there are kids that happen to have a low grade and have missing assignments. We'll see, but I highly doubt it, except there is one kid who is borderline.

I'm just thinking, I have downtime in this moment and am wondering what to do? I feel myself wanting to revert to bad habits and tell myself to keep working on lesson plans and quizzes for the first book we are covering for the fall semester. I already finished the first fall semester test yesterday. Now I'm pressing and thinking I should work on the quizzes for the first book and work on a second week of lesson plans, even though I have nothing to do tomorrow if no kids show up and I could do it then.

I realize, once I grade the tests and essays from today, with the remaining time I need to do something for myself rather than push hard to prep for the fall semester. If I choose to do nothing for the rest of this period and tomorrow that is school related, that is ok, and I need to be ok with that. I have done so much already. My focus needs to be how I am going to enjoy my three weeks off and have fun, spend time with friends, go golfing. What I don't need to do, that I used to do a lot in my past, is catch up on all the household stuff that needs to be done. If I happen to feel the urge to do that, what is more important is, like my teaching, to set up an infrastructure on what needs to be done, how to do it and timeframes; much like my workouts.

Think long-term planning, short-term execution where it helps me not to be stressed or feel pressure over it. That is something to consider with my down time. I started to think about what it's going to be like when I step into the classroom with full classes and a full schedule. For the first time in a long time, I thought about the future without feeling terrified. I actually felt some hope based on the work and investing of myself. I was finally starting to learn to not put myself on the backburner.

A month later, I got a letter in the mail with my classroom assignments. I was teaching two honors classes, and my third period was going to be my prep period. My biggest class was going to be 24 and my smallest class of 15. It's not a bad mixture.

Before I knew it, the month passed by, we had our start of the school year pre-meetings, and we had our first day of orientation. That morning, I stepped in my classroom, and even though everything I had been through, and the three years removed, it felt like I never left. It was a weird comfortable feeling.

That morning passed like a flash. At the end of the school day, I sat my desk to check my emails. Before that, I suddenly just stared out

Chapter Thirty-Two

of the window behind me. I looked down the road, and most of the school cleared out so there were few cars, then I looked up at the ridge where the old Navy barracks used to be and where the Coyotes hung out. I never saw them during the day but after supervising an evening volleyball or basketball game, and as I was waiting for the last kids to be picked up, I heard them howling from that direction.

I stared out of the window. I was in one piece. I did not fall apart, I did not feel any tingling or suddenly a drop in my stomach that I was dropping in the "Oh No" zone. I felt a sense of peace. Teaching did not drive me into that mental facility. I did.

I watched a "30 for 30" sports documentary about Ricky Williams. He stated something to the effect that he stopped blaming his parents for what happened to him when he was a kid. He said that if you keep blaming your parents for the things they do, then you give them the power to change things instead of yourself. He went on to say that through his study of yoga, that stress does not just happen to us, we create our own stress.

I thought about that. Then I received a text from my wife with heart emojis saying she loves me, misses me, and hopes my day went well. I gave the kissing emoji back to her. It was good to feel that maybe my wife and psychiatrist are right, that I am not going to end up back in a mental facility. I took a deep breath in and realized that maybe today was a first step in that direction.

EPILOGUE

After that realization, the reality, as far as going forward, was that dealing and coping with my mental health issues were not going to be all puppy dogs and ice cream. There were moments were I could not make heads or tails because of the diverse diagnosis from different psychiatrists. So when I would get tingly or think that I was having an "oh, no" moment, instead of being terrified I was now still scared but also confused because I did not know if it was my bipolar or anxiety disorder. Even though I continued my wellness journey as far as fitness and nutrition, wellness through mediation, and taking my meds as needed, I realized a month later, it was not a warranty or guarantee of not having an episode.

About a month later, around the middle of September, I did have an episode. I was not sure if it was work related, but I have a tendency to overwork myself, which was slightly happening but it was more that I was frustrated with my weight loss which is a completely different story on its own, but I seemed to hit a wall or what we call a weight loss plateau.

At this point in time, I had lost 34 pounds. I wanted to achieve two goals – to lose 35 pounds while at the same time breaking 220 – and it just was not happening. To help myself, I decided to do two things, which was to make a second appointment with a nutritionist and work out two times a day. I should have known better about working out twice a day because it was bound to affect my sleep which was a big contributor to my manic episode.

I would get up at 4:30 am, go workout, go through my work day, come home and change and workout in the afternoon at 4:45 pm. I did that for about a week and it worked because I ended up losing 9 pounds so I was right back at 220. But I did pay a price for it.

I woke up my wife and told her my thoughts were racing and my medication was not kicking in that I took before I went to bed. I was so scared that I called the helpline through my health insurance and told the person on the line what was going on, and she asked me if I was hearing voices or if I wanted to hurt myself. I told her no. We talked further, and she asked me if anyone was there with me. I said yes. She then said if I felt out of control and that if I can't calm my mind that it would be best to go to the emergency room and request a psychiatrist to evaluate me. She emphasized to have my wife take me; if not she would call 911 for me to come pick me up to go to the hospital.

It took me a moment, but I started to calm down. That was about 12:30 a.m. or so. But what calmed me down was she said go to the hospital to get evaluated, she did not say to go to be placed on another hold, and it really had a calming effect though after I hung up with her. I was still terrified and honestly I was one step away from telling my wife to take me to the hospital. Then after talking to her for about 20 minutes, my medication started to kick in and I calmed down even more. And I was feeling ready to go to sleep but I was definitely going to call in sick for the next few days.

The next night I was having a bit of the same struggle. I took my medication and had a really good sleep until around 2:16 in the morning. I didn't mess around; I took my medication right away. I was having a lot of fears and turned on my sleep meditation to try to fall back asleep; it worked a little bit at first, but it was happening again as far as these worse case scenarios running in and out of my mind. I then did something I had not done before. First of all, I did not wake up my wife right away. Then, I took on my fears head on and told my fears about what was not going to happen.

I took each fear one step at a time. For example, one fear that was coming up, what happens if I have an episode at school again? I then thought about a contingency plan if did happen. So, I thought about what the lady said to me on the helpline that whatever happens that evening if I decide to go to the hospital, to not drive myself. So, I thought, Monday I will go in and talk to my work buddy, Greg, and tell him what happened and that I'm okay. I'm well rested, and I took my meds, but if I start to have an episode I will call him and ask him to take me to the ER to get evaluated. Just that simple thought put my mind completely at ease and I was able to fall back to sleep.

That was September 2022. Even though it was tough to go through that episode, I was optimistic going forward that I could handle what was going to be thrown my way as far as my mental health challenges. Things were going very smoothly. I had met with my psychiatrist and told him that I was living my best life. I was spending more time with friends and golfing more. I was investing in myself instead of putting myself on the backburner. Everything was awesome until about Thanksgiving 2023. I was putting myself through a lot of stress.

About a week before Thanksgiving, and I think it was a Wednesday. I walked down from my classroom right before I was going to start tutoring to go into the teacher's lounge. A student I had taught the year before, yelled out my nickname, "Hey Hecman!" for everyone to hear. Of course, he was showing off in front of his friends. For those that are not teachers, calling a teacher by their first name is not good. So, instead of embarrassing him in front of his friends, I pulled him aside and told him he could not do that.

I thought the kid would be reasonable and would just leave it at that. The very next day, as I was heading up the stairs to start after school tutoring, he decided to call me by my first name again. I gave him a glare, but I made sure I didn't react to him. So after I wrapped up tutoring, I wrote him two detention slips to spend two days after school thinking about his disrespect.

The next day, I pulled him out class and privately gave him the detention slips. Honestly, I thought this shit would be done after that. But it got worse. I was on lunchtime supervision duty and he and his group of friends were calling me by my first name. It didn't stop there. When I walked through campus, every boy from his graduating class would cat call me by my first name. The last straw for me was when I was walking to my car after school. There was football practice going on and just before I got in my car, one of the football players called out my first name. I stormed over to the practice field. I could not prove who did it, but I knew it was either the sophomore boys, because they were friends with this kid that started this whole shit storm, or they were egging a freshman on to do it.

I approached the football coach and told him that one of his players called my first name out and that I found it very disrespectful.

He didn't even look at me, he had his eyes glued to his phone, and said, "How do you know it was one of my players?"

I was disappointed and disgusted how he handled it because being a former coach, I know I would have ran those players until they puked or until one of them would admit they said it. So, that was it for me trying to handle this on my own. I made a list of students that were around when I was being cat called by my first name. I then emailed the principal and the dean to inform them that I was being harassed, attached the list with dates and time, and told them it is beginning to affect my mental health.

To their credit, they handled it very well, and it never happened again. I didn't relaize it in the moment, but it took a toll on me. The damage was done as far as trying to cope with my stress on my own. The stress carried over into December because the students were getting anxious with the Winter break coming up in a couple of weeks.

I should have seen the signs. I was not having trouble going to sleep, but when I had to go to the bathroom in the middle of the night, I was having trouble going back to sleep. It got worse because my birthday was coming up and my wife planned a big party, so then there was the adrenaline and excitement kicking in.

It was my birthday, so of course I called in sick and I got to sleep in, had breakfast and headed to the gym. Just as I finished my workout, I headed to my car and suddenly I felt this rush of adrenaline and then it turned to euphoria that was starting to scare me because it was rising like a giant wave, almost to tsunami proportions. I thought maybe because it was I had a great workout and the excitement of this party that my wife planned for me. But the elevation of my mood would not stop. It felt very similar to the beginnings of the manic episode I had four years ago.

I didn't mess around. I hopped in my car and headed to the emergency room. I called my wife and told her I was headed there and to stay on the phone with me in case I started to lose my sense of direction, which I did because I had to tell my wife landmarks in order to get me there because my brain circuits were scrambled. Once I got close, I had to pull over so I could get a temporary hold on my senses to see that I was going in the right direction.

Once I got to the emergency room, I simply gave my phone to the nurse and my wife walked her through what was going on, and once she got the information to check me in, and she put a red wrist band on me. I felt a bit of calm come over and I sat down and talked to my wife and she said she was going to call our daughter and head over to ER and wait with me for the psychiatrist to evaluate me.

After about thirty minutes, my wife got there with our daughter, and they gave me a big hug. My wife would tell me later that this episode was much different than it was four years before because I was not pacing back and forth or looked like I was trying to crawl out of my skin. The nurse told us that they had a lot of psychiatric patients and that it would take several hours, then she said, "By the way, happy birthday. I'm sorry you have to be in here today."

I turned to my daughter and told her that I was okay and that she could go because she would sit being bored. She then gave me a hug and headed out to whatever plans she had.

It was about three hours before I was called in and really it was more to check my vitals and state of mind. The doctor that evaluated me said to us "You don't seem manic to me." I was already calmed after waiting three hours, but that was a huge relief. Even though my mind was still a bit scrambled, and I was still a bit edgy, I felt really confident that there was no way that I was going back to that mental facility. I felt really good and saying that and I looked at my wife and without me saying anything I just knew she knew what I was feeling and thinking in that moment. I just felt like there were signs all around that I was going to recover from this a lot quicker than four years ago and I will be well from this latest episode.

Another, probably about two hours had passed. Now we were going on five hours before I was called in.

I looked at my wife and said, "Thank God, I'm starving. Let's go have some Jack in the Box tacos after this."

She laughed at that.

We walked toward one of the rooms, and I saw the number on the door and pointed to my wife and said, "Look, 47."

She said, "Whoa. That's a sign," as 47 was my football number in college. Man, outside of being a husband and a dad, those were some of the best times I have ever had in my life.

Two hours later, the psychiatrist came in. I recognized him right away, his name was Dr. Hill.

"I remember you," I said. "Four years ago you told me that I should have went on a 72-hour hold and I didn't listen. The next day I landed right back in the ER."

He recognized me and my wife, and we carried on for about 20 minutes. He then told my wife that this was more of a hyperactive episode than manic. He told us that sometimes bipolar, general anxiety disorder, and ADHD can have similar symptoms, and it is hard to distinguish from one another. I felt great that it was not a manic episode. He then said that the current anxiety medication is not strong enough. He said to forgive him for the analogy but the current medicine was more like Tylenol and that I needed the Oxycodone version for my anxiety. He told me it was very important to get my medication ASAP then to get right to bed and rest. I thanked him and said, "So I'm good to go get some tacos?"

"Only after you get your medication, but yeah you are good to go. And if you need to talk to someone right away, here is my card."

"Thanks Doc," I said. Then I looked at my wife. "Talk about signs."

"I know. Talk about divine intervention. This being on your birthday, the room number, you and the doc talking like you are bosom buddies."

"Yeah, I know, and this time around, someone was definitely looking after me."

Of course, afterwards I did get my tacos, and some large curly fries too.

It was New Year's Eve, and we had plans to go have dinner that night and we were staying at a hotel where they had a view of the harbor where the *Queen Mary* was docked, and they were going to let off fireworks at midnight. Before we packed and left, we had our usual weekend breakfast, which was a homemade breakfast burrito. My wife made them simple, just scrambled eggs, cheese, and some hot sauce wrapped in a flour tortilla – on paper, nothing special, but she made them so good, and we would have a cup of decaf coffee. We would then just chit-chat about life and our future plans, but I was unusually quiet for about 15 minutes.

My wife noticed. "What's up?"

"What do you mean?"

"You've been very quiet and I've been doing all the talking."

"I was thinking about a movie I just saw," I said. I was off the past week for Christmas break and binge watching some shows. As scrolling through Netflix, I saw this movie with Bradley Cooper called *The Silver Linings Playbook*. Jennifer Lawrence was also in it. The movie was about a guy who was being releases from a mental hospital because he had a manic episode to where he almost beat a man to death. The movie is about how he coped with life once he was released and back home.

One of the mistakes he made when he got home was he tried to cope with his mental health challenges by not taking his meds and keeping himself busy. His goal was to win back his wife, who sold the house and left him while he was in the mental hospital. She was an English teacher, and one of the first things he was going to do was read all the books she had on her syllabus that she gave to her students in the beginning of the school year. After a while, he saw that trying to win his wife back was becoming an exercise in futility. His parents set a boundary and told him he had to take his meds and continue his therapy or he would have to go back to the mental hospital. Even though he was reluctant, he did take his meds, go to therapy, and through the help of Jennifer Lawrence's character was able to center himself and cope with his life better.

After giving some background of the story, I told her how that story hit home for me, especially the fact that he was able to move forward without his wife and he had become more productive and centered because he asked for help. I thought that was an amazing act of courage when you consider that thirty percent of people with bipolar disorder end up committing suicide.

I told my wife that I'm lucky I consider myself in the seventy percent group that is not just surviving but thriving despite this challenge. I told her about the scene when Bradley Cooper's character loses his shit the first time. The first book he read from his wife's list was *A Farewell to Arms* by Ernest Hemingway. He spent one entire evening reading the book and finished it at 3 am. Then he chucked the book out of a plate glass window when he was done. He woke up his parents to tell them how frustrated he was about the tragic ending.

When I had that thought, it then rolled over to the inscription for Hemingway's novel, *For Whom the Bell Tolls* where it talks about no man being an island.

Before we headed to check into the hotel for New Years, my wife had to run some errands. While she was gone, I thought more about our breakfast conversation more, to the point that I felt I had to sit and journal other thoughts that were now flooding my mind.

I kept thinking over and over again how lucky am I that I feel confident that I am part of that seventy percent. For the rest of my life, I will work hard at keeping myself there, but I cannot do it without help.

I then thought about the thirty percent who succumb to taking their own lives. I especially thought of country music legend Naomi Judd. It was so sad that she committed suicide. But more sad how much pain and suffering she must have been going through in order to even have that gun in her hand to shoot herself. I am theorizing that she felt guilty about telling her story, to ask for help. She was probably so worried about being judged or judging herself so harshly or both, that it led her to believe she was not worthy enough to be saved from all that suffering. Cookie was also part of that thirty percent, but the only difference was, she did it slowly with drugs.

Then I thought about a line from a movie called *A River Runs Through It*. One of characters is talking to her love interest about the frustration she was experiencing with her brother who was recently visiting from California. She then says, "Why is it the people who need the most help...won't take it?"

In reality, that's the only difference between the thirty percent and the seventy percent. Reaching for help and telling your story. If you don't, you create that lonely, dreaded island mentioned in the inscription in the Hemingway book. I then think about the movie *Castaway* with Tom Hanks as the lead character. Sorry, spoil alert coming. He decided after spending four years on a deserted island he had the realization that no one was coming to get him. In those four years, he developed an imaginary friend in the form of a volleyball named Wilson. He built a raft and told Wilson that he'd rather try and make it than stay on that island with him.

That is the difference. When you create a shithole island, you either are going to be the thirty percent who wait and die or the seventy percent who take a chance on life on their own terms and have the hope that help is out there. Like Tom Hanks' character, if I can help it, and for the rest of my life, that is not an island I want to be on.

ACKNOWLEDGEMENTS

First and foremost, I need to acknowledge my editors, Nancy Albright and Rob Bignell. To Nancy who believed in my manuscript from day one. I sent excerpts of my memoir to twenty different editors before Nancy contacted me that she wanted to work with me on the manuscript. Her suggestions, her experience, and our bond over rock music made her an invaluable asset in seeing the completion of my manuscript.

I also would like to acknowledge Ms. Laura Tohe, my poetry professor at Arizona State University. I took the class as an elective, and I thought it would be an easy "A." Little did I know that class would change my life. Most importantly, she was the first person in my life to tell me that I was talented at something.

To all my peers and professors in the MFA program at Cal State Long Beach, especially my mentor Dr. Gerald Locklin, a true role model who believed that I deserve to be in the Master's Program, who believed I could graduate from the MFA program, and believed I could be published.

To Vinnie Corbo and Volossal Publishing for believing in me.

To all my colleagues at Junipero Serra High School, St. Pius/Matthias Academy, and Mary Star of the Sea High School, who grounded me, supported me, respected me, and most importantly could make me laugh during a tough day or tough faculty meeting.

For all the students I taught, who encouraged me over and over that I should write a book. Thank you, especially to those who would send me late night emails from college while they were working on an all-nighter essay, thanking me for supporting them and believing in them when they were just discovering the first steps of who they were.

Last but not least, my incredible support group, my family, therapists, my therapy groups, my psychiatrists, especially Dr. Aguilar and Dr. Hind who always reassured me that I had a great chance of not ending up in a mental hospital again.

To my stepmom Irene, who is a saint and the greatest undiscovered cook in the world. She is the bedrock of the Rivera family. To my brothers who always kept me honest, and all my sister and brother-in-laws, who are always fun to be around.

To all my homies from El Co, ASU, Al, Pao, Rob, Moheni, Scott and Kenny, Big Vince, Shelly, Julianna, Damon, and my roommates I had over the years, especially Rudy, Frank, Jeff and George. My brother-in-law Brian and my nephew Hunter who have great stories about the West Side and Culvers. A special thanks to Le and Glenna Hoff, who showed every day that age is nothin' but a number."

To my dad, who taught me the importance of being a man, a good husband, and a good father.

And of course, to my lovely daughter who would give the shirt off her back for anyone.

And finally, my wife, so much I can say that I could write another book. She is the greatest good I ever will have in my life, and taught me the value of humor. Besides, no matter what crazy idea I had, she always said, "You should go for it!"

ABOUT THE AUTHOR

Hector Rivera was born in Perth Amboy, New Jersey to a Boricua Mother (Puerto Rican) and Peruvian Father. He sees himself as a warrior, philosopher and poet. He has won awards playing football in high school and college. He received his Masters of Fine Arts in Creative Writing with an emphasis on poetry from Long Beach State. He received Honorable Mention in the San Gabriel Valley Poetry Contest in April 2000.

As a high school teacher, he has won several educational awards; including Teacher of the Year in 2008 and 2009. He is currently in his 23rd year of teaching and loves spending time with his wife, daughter, family, friends and obsessively listening

photo by Pablo Rivera

to music and watching sports. He says he does not drink sangria or have a crystal ball but plans to see as many Def Leppard concerts as possible and hopes to watch the Yankees win their 30th championship before he "kicks the bucket."

www.ingramcontent.com/pod-product-compliance
Lightning Source LLC
Chambersburg PA
CBHW032044150426
43194CB00006B/413